Best wishes

Colin Sproston

12/2007

NOBLE CURIOS & CONNECTIONS

About the Author

Colin Sproston was born on a farm near Rugeley in mid-Staffordshire. He is the fourth generation Sproston to be born in Staffordshire, the previous seven generations having been born just across the border in Cheshire.

After Rugeley Grammar School, he gained a B.Sc. (Hons) in Chemistry from the University College of Wales, Aberystwyth.

Much of his working life was spent with subsidiaries and associates of The General Electric Company, p.l.c, during which time he qualified as a Chartered Management Accountant and a Chartered Certified Accountant. From 1983 to 1996, he was Finance Director of GEC Meters Limited following which he joined ALSTOM as a Vice-President, Finance & Administration. From August 2000, he was Finance Director of Morrell Products Limited before retiring in 2006.

He is married, has two sons and still lives in semi-rural Staffordshire.

This book is a product of his long-standing interest in local history.

Noble Curios & Connections

A Beginner's Guide to the Aristocracy and Landed Gentry of Staffordshire and elsewhere in the form of Aristocratic Curios plus Interesting and Intriguing Facts

COLIN SPROSTON

Order this book online at www.trafford.com/06-1088
or email orders@trafford.com

Most Trafford titles are also available at major online book retailers.

Note for Librarians: A cataloguing record for this book is available from Library
and Archives Canada at www.collectionscanada.ca/amicus/index-e.html

Printed in Victoria, BC, Canada.

ISBN: 978-1-4120-9334-7

*We at Trafford believe that it is the responsibility of us all, as both individuals
and corporations, to make choices that are environmentally and socially sound.
You, in turn, are supporting this responsible conduct each time you purchase a
Trafford book, or make use of our publishing services. To find out how you are
helping, please visit www.trafford.com/responsiblepublishing.html*

*Our mission is to efficiently provide the world's finest, most comprehensive
book publishing service, enabling every author to experience success.
To find out how to publish your book, your way, and have it available
worldwide, visit us online at www.trafford.com/10510*

www.trafford.com

North America & international
toll-free: 1 888 232 4444 (USA & Canada)
phone: 250 383 6864 ♦ fax: 250 383 6804
email: info@trafford.com

The United Kingdom & Europe
phone: +44 (0)1865 722 113 ♦ local rate: 0845 230 9601
facsimile: +44 (0)1865 722 868 ♦ email: info.uk@trafford.com

10 9 8 7 6 5 4 3 2

This book is dedicated to
Sue, my wife
Richard and Andrew, our two children
I am grateful for their understanding and support

Contents

APPENDICES:

Acknowledgements

There are many people I would like to acknowledge for giving me the inspiration to write this book.

These include, in no particular order:

My parents, who were both members of large families with substantial Staffordshire and Shropshire connections. They and other family members provided me with a lot of background to some of the families and places I have written about in this book;

Mr E C Toye, my history master at Rugeley Grammar School. He was always affectionately known as "Chus" on account of his mispronunciation of Massachusetts. He nurtured my interest in history, in particular, local history;

My wife, Sue, and my two sons, Richard and Andrew, who have had to put up with my lengthy disappearances into my 'study', to various libraries or places mentioned in this book. They have also encouraged me when the spark seemed to be going out;

Henry Hobhouse for showing how an unusual slant on facts can be both stimulating and interesting – a review of his book "Seeds of Wealth" in the Spectator sums up his approach: "You cannot help but admire and enjoy the company of a man who takes such a novel and global view of history";

Hugh Montgomery Massingberd for his stimulating and evocative books and his past articles in the Daily Telegraph on the subject of country houses;

The subjects of this book, who made this work possible as well as interesting;

All the people whose articles and books I have referenced;

All the other people, who contributed in some way to make the compilation of this book possible.

Introduction

This book comprises a small trivia trove of anecdotes combined with some more serious information about people from noble families and the landed gentry as well as the consequences of belonging to such families. The result is that members of the peerage mingle with baronets, who also have hereditary titles, and people who never achieved a hereditary title. The chapter titles reflect some aspect of the content even if irrelevant to the main subject.

My intention was to put together a series of notes in such a way to enable the reader to pick up the book, open it almost anywhere and start reading. As a result, this has necessarily led to some repetition of facts, which, hopefully, does not detract from the overall appreciation of the book.

Consequently, the main text of each chapter has been kept relatively brief. However, each chapter has been supplemented by some further comments under the heading "Further Notes and Connections". These notes sometimes meander from the main text but prevent the latter from becoming too cluttered.

As the header page to this book suggests, it was my intention to put together a collection of miscellaneous facts sometimes linking the various families I have written about - I hope that you will find something interesting somewhere within the following pages.

The idea for such a collection of aristocratic trivia struck me whilst I was reading a book review of Imperial Vanities, written by Brian Thompson. I have always been interested in aristocracy and their impact on British society and, although the following little pieces of aristocratic trivia are not intended to be of any historical import, I hope that they may stimulate you to delve deeper into the rich history of the United Kingdom as I did in researching this book with particular reference to my home county of Staffordshire.

The book has been arranged to allow the reader just to dip into – either directly into the main chapter texts or the 'Further Notes and Connections', appended to each chapter, which, in the main, can be read independently. In some cases, where there are many interesting related facts, the Further Notes and Connections are more extensive than their preceding chapters.

During these aristocratic ramblings, other incidental pieces of trivia fall out, which may answer or partly answer some questions you may have considered in the past – for example, what is the 'Lizard' in Weston-under-Lizard?

I have also tried to highlight connections, which many people may not be aware of – for example, the same family once owned Lilleshall Hall (in the grounds of which is the National Sports Centre) and Trentham Gardens. Or, that Staffordshire was the end of the road for most of the Gunpowder Plot conspirators. Some of the connections are within a single chapter; in others, the connections span two or more chapters

The origins of the aristocracy as we know it today go back to 1066 and the Norman Conquest, when the Anglo-Saxon élite was swept away and replaced by Norman supporters of William I, who were given large tracts of land formerly owned by Anglo-Saxon lords. By 1086, as revealed in the Domesday Book, only four members of the old English ruling class were still in possession of their land; over 4,000 pre-Conquest thegns had been dispossessed and England was now in the hands of fewer than 200 new barons. The next event to have a major impact on the aristocracy was the Dissolution of the Monasteries. In the 1540s and early 1550s, a quarter of the land of England passed from institutional hands to private hands, which profoundly affected the evolution of English Landed Society until the end of the 19th century. During this period, the arrival of the Industrial Revolution was initially favourable to the aristocracy, particularly to those who were able to exploit the wealth on or beneath their extensive land holdings and those who invested in the development of the country's transport infrastructure. Such Staffordshire families included the Littletons, the Pagets and the Leveson-Gowers. However, it could be said that the Industrial Revolution sowed the seeds, which ultimately led to erosion of the power of the aristocracy. One eventual side effect of this power shift was the demise of the English Country House, which is discussed later.

Wherever you live in the United Kingdom, there is almost certainly going to be some local noble family, which has had an impact on the development of the area. In fact, in some cases, such families may still be influential in the area. One only has to think of the Duke of Westminster - besides his major property holdings in London, he still has substantial influence around Chester, close to his home at Eaton Hall.

I also hope that the Appendices will provide some help in placing the families in the context of the history of Staffordshire and, indeed, in some cases, that of England and the United Kingdom.

Appendix 1 gives a brief summary of hereditary titles and order of precedence.

As a proud man of Staffordshire, I have placed the emphasis of this book on people with Staffordshire connections such as the Earls of Shrewsbury, the Marquess of Anglesey, the Earls of Harrowby, the Earls of Lichfield, the Leveson-Gowers (Dukes of Sutherland and Earls Granville), Lord Stafford's antecedents, the Lords Hatherton, Sir Charles Wolseley, the Astons/Cliffords and the Harpur-Crewes. Another legacy these people have left behind is in the names of public houses and roads, a few examples of which are given in Appendix 2. In addition, for a land-locked county, which is just about as far away as one can be from the sea, Staffordshire has produced a surprising number of sailors, who reached the upper echelons of the Royal Navy. Some of these sailors are mentioned in this book including Admiral Anson, the 18th Earl of Shrewsbury, John Jervis (Earl St Vincent) and Admiral Leveson-Gower. I do not claim that this book covers all of the aristocratic families associated with Staffordshire nor, necessarily, all of the important families. The families discussed are those with whom I have been familiar for many years through various interests.

As might be expected with a discourse on the nobility and the landed gentry, the country house often looms large. Regrettably, this is now too often just a memory, as many of these houses have disappeared. A brief treatise on the demise of the country house is given in Appendix 3. You will also see that some of Staffordshire's country houses have literary associations, including such famous authors as P G Wodehouse and J R R Tolkien as well as lesser-known authors, and a strong link to a well-known mediaeval story, 'Sir Gawain and the Green Knight'.

You do not have to be a lover of the aristocracy and what it stands for, or probably more correctly nowadays, what it stood for. However, whether you like it or not, members of aristocratic families have played an important role in our history at both national and local levels.

Appendices 4 and 5 provide a brief introduction to two families with strong Staffordshire connections, members of which appear in some of the main chapters.

Scattered throughout this book are references to the great offices of state in England and Scotland, which, although now mainly of a ceremonial nature, were, historically, very important positions. There is a brief description of the English offices in Appendix 6 along with a table of some Staffordshire people, who have held these positions.

Appendix 7 is a short treatise on the Dissolution of the Monasteries and the Reformation, the former providing fortunes, or substantially enhancing them, for many families, including some in this book.

Appendix 8 is a concise dictionary of terms and abbreviations that one is likely to come across when researching old documents.

As an aid to placing the subjects of this book in an historical context, Appendix 9 provides a list of Kings, Queens and Rulers of England. It should be noted that even lists of kings and queens are subject to argument over who should be included and the dates of their reigns.

Appendix 10 is a brief discussion of the impact of the Industrial Revolution and the development of the country's transport infrastructure and the involvement of many Staffordshire people. You will also note that, in the late 18th century, Staffordshire was very much in the vanguard of agricultural development as well as that of industry.

I am aware of many other noble/aristocratic/landed families with Staffordshire connections, which could be the subject of another such book; these include the Legges (Earls of Dartmouth), the Wards (Earls of Dudley), the Sneyds (Keele Hall), the Wrottesleys, the Giffards (Chillington Hall), the Meynell-Ingrams (Hoar Cross Hall), the Bagots (Blithfield Hall) and the Moncktons (Stretton Hall and Somerford Hall) to name but a few. The few brief notes on some of these families in Appendix 11 provide a taster to such a book.

In the course of my research for this book, it has frequently been proved to me that one has to check the accuracy of documents referred to. Despite my best endeavours, I cannot guarantee that some of the information I have extracted from other documents does not perpetuate errors found within them. Nevertheless, I have found the act of verification has been very stimulating, even though I have not always been successful in bringing these to a satisfactory conclusion. It has also been very satisfying to solve some mysteries and fill in gaps.

You will also observe that spelling variations frequently appear – English spellings were not regularised until relatively recent times – even now, there are differences between British spellings and American spellings as well as differences in pronunciation and word usage. In general, British spellings have been used in this book.

PART 1
STAFFORDSHIRE FAMILIES

A Family Of Influence

There have been few examples of such a steady rise to power of one family. In a century and half, the Leveson-Gowers had eclipsed all the old families of the past in Staffordshire; each generation adding titles and wealth. In the 18th century, the landed aristocracy formed the ruling class of England; by the end of that century, there were few of the ruling families of England, which were not descended from or allied to the Leveson-Gowers.

It all started with two families - the Levesons (*pronounced Looson*) and the Gowers (*pronounced Gore*). The Levesons were known to be settled in Willenhall, Staffordshire, by the 13th century and, by the reign of Elizabeth I (1553-1603), they were among the leading woolstaplers (merchants) in the neighbouring town of Wolverhampton.[1,2] They had acquired monastic lands after the Dissolution of the Monasteries: Trentham [3] in Staffordshire (1540) and Lilleshall [4] in Shropshire (1543).

In 1588, Admiral Sir Richard Leveson took part in the action against the Spanish Armada.

In 1631, Frances Leveson, daughter and heiress of Sir John Leveson (1598-1661) married Sir Thomas Gower, 2nd Baronet, of Stittenham, a few miles north-east of York and close to Castle Howard. Sir Thomas and Frances had a son, William Leveson Gower *(pronounced Looson-Gore)*, who became the 4th Baronet. He further improved the family's status and wealth by marrying Lady Jane Granville, daughter and heiress of the 1st Earl of Bath. Their son, John, was created 1st Baron Gower by Queen Anne. He married Catherine Manners, daughter of the 1st Duke of Rutland. He was succeeded by his son, John (1675 - 1709).

On 8 July 1746, Sir John Leveson-Gower, 2nd Lord Gower was created 1st Viscount Trentham and 1st Earl Gower for supporting the Hanoverians against the Jacobite rebellion. His first marriage to Lady Evelyn Pierrepoint, daughter of the 1st Duke of Kingston, produced 10 children. Later, he married Penelope, daughter of John Stonehouse; she had one child who died in infancy. Finally, he married Mary, daughter of the 6th Earl of Thanet, and had a further four children.[5] He changed sides from Tory to Whig after Gertrude, one of his daughters, married the 4th Duke of Bedford in 1737.[6] It was this act that led Samuel Johnson, the famous lexicographer who was born in Lichfield, Staffordshire, to define a Gower as a turncoat.[7] His third son, Granville, succeeded as the 2nd Earl in 1754, as his two elder brothers had died.

Granville Leveson-Gower (1721-1803), the 2nd Earl Gower, was educated at Westminster and Christ Church, Oxford. He became an MP for Bishop's Castle, Shropshire, then Westminster and later Lichfield. He was Lord of the Admiralty from 1749 to 1751. When his father died, Granville entered the House of Lords and held a number of posts including Lord Privy Seal from 1755-1757 and Lord President of the Council from 1767-1769. The 2nd Earl Gower was also an entrepreneur, who was a major contributor to the rise of modern industry within Staffordshire and the West Midlands.[8]

On 1 March 1786, the 2nd Earl Gower was created Marquess of Stafford by George III as a reward for political services. He married three times.[9] His second wife, Lady Louisa Egerton, whom he married in 1754, was daughter of Scrope Egerton, the 1st Duke of Bridgewater. Under the terms of the will of the 3rd Duke of Bridgewater, who had no direct heirs, Louisa's eldest son, George Granville Leveson-Gower, enjoyed the proceeds from his estate for one generation. Thereafter, the income went to her second son, Francis.

Granville and Louisa's eldest son, George Granville Leveson-Gower, (1758-1833) succeeded as the 2nd Marquess of Stafford in 1803. George married Elizabeth, Countess of Sutherland (1765-1839), who inherited a million acres in Scotland. She was a countess in her own right.[10] In 1833, the year of his death, George was created 1st Duke of Sutherland by William IV, the title being chosen for him by his wife. His wife thereafter became known as the Duchess-Countess.[11]

George had been educated at Westminster and Christ Church, Oxford. He became an MP for Newcastle under Lyme in 1778 and 1780 and MP for Staffordshire from 1787 to 1798. He was ambassador to Paris from 1790 to 1792, during which the French Revolution took place. In addition to possessing his huge estate in Sutherland through his wife, he inherited the Bridgewater estates from his uncle, Francis Egerton, the 3rd and last Duke of Bridgewater [12], and on the death of his father, the estates of Stittenham (Yorkshire), Trentham (Staffordshire), Lilleshall (Shropshire) and the remaining properties around Wolverhampton, then still part of Staffordshire. George became a controversial figure because of the Highland Clearances, which were undertaken in the period from 1812 to 1820. However, he made substantial improvements in Sutherland by building 450 miles of roads and 134 bridges between 1812 and 1832. The 1st Duke has been called in a book title, 'The Leviathan of Wealth'. He is believed to have had an annual income of £200,000, roughly the equivalent of £14 million per annum in 2003.

In 1827, George purchased Stafford House in London. This property, next to Clarence House in London, was built in the 1820s for George IV's brother, the Duke of York. George bought a 100-year lease on the property. In 1913, it was sold to Sir Harold Lever, later Lord Leverhulme, the founder of the business that became Unilever. He changed its name to Lancaster House and then gave the remainder of the lease to the government. It is now used by the government for entertaining foreign leaders and other similar events.

The 2nd Duke, also called George Granville Leveson Gower, was born in 1786 and died in 1861. In 1823, he married Harriet Elizabeth Georgiana Howard (1806-1868), daughter of the 6th Earl of Carlisle and his wife Georgiana Dorothy Cavendish; her grandfather was the 5th Duke of Devonshire. She was brought up at Castle Howard in Yorkshire. She was Mistress of the Robes for various periods between 1837 and 1861 and a great friend of Queen Victoria. Harriet was a driving force behind the rebuilding of Trentham by Sir Charles Barry, the architect of the House of Commons. It is estimated that the couple spent £60,000 on Dunrobin in Scotland, £50,000 on Cliveden [13], £275,000 on Stafford House as well as £260,000 on Trentham. As a comparison, 2003 costs would be approximately 75 times higher! The 2nd Duke was very deaf and so did not become involved in politics. Harriet was only 17 when they married and she had 11 children, 8 of whom survived. Three of their daughters married Dukes.

The 3rd Duke was George Granville William Leveson-Gower (1828-1892). His first wife was Ann Hay-Mackenzie, Countess of Cromartie (1829-1888). He succeeded to the dukedom in 1861 having been MP for Sutherland from 1852. [14] The 3rd Duke was having an affair with Mary Blair, nee Mitchell, before his first wife died. He married Mary only three months after becoming a widower - a scandal at the time. On his death in 1892, he tried to leave Mary that part of the estate that was not entailed. The 4th Duke challenged the will. Mary was sent to prison for six weeks for contempt of court for burning a document. In the end she agreed to be paid off with the sum of £500,000 in cash. For this the Bank of England printed 500 notes of £1000 denomination to make the transfer after which the notes were destroyed.

The 3rd Duke's son, Cromartie Sutherland Leveson-Gower (1852-1913), who succeeded as the 4th Duke, married Millicent St. Claire Erskine (1867-1955).[15] The couple had four children, the first died aged 2.

George Granville Sutherland Leveson-Gower (1888-1963), the 5th Duke, married twice but had no children.[16] His younger brother, Alistair, who died in his 20s had only a daughter, Elizabeth Millicent Sutherland Leveson-Gower, who inherited the title of 24th Countess of Sutherland when the 5th Duke died. The Dukedom passed to John Sutherland Egerton, 5th Earl of Ellesmere and great-great grandson of Francis Sutherland-Leveson-Gower, 1st Earl of Ellesmere (and younger son of the 1st Duke of Sutherland), who had assumed the name Egerton.[17] Francis Roland Egerton, the 6th Duke's first cousin once removed, became the 7th Duke of Sutherland in 2000.

A Family Of Influence
Further Notes And Connections

1. In the 13th century, Wolverhampton became a prosperous market town catering for the surrounding area. Good roads would have been an essential requirement for the development of the market town and Wolverhampton must have developed many links with the Welsh border country to the west, which was home to some of the best sheep in the country. Over the next century, Wolverhampton's fortunes continued to improve and the town became wealthy from the wool trade. Wool was purchased by the local wool merchants, such as the Levesons, and sold on to Europe, where it was used by clothing manufacturers.

2. Ashmore Hall and the Ashmore Park estate were sold by the Leveson-Gowers in the early 1700s; further Wolverhampton properties were sold in 1739 to a Mr Charles Osborn, a Wolverhampton Quaker, for £5,000.

3. The Augustinian Priory at Trentham (said to have been founded in 1150 by the 2nd Earl of Chester) had acquired considerable surrounding lands, stretching northwards towards what is now the town of Newcastle-under-Lyme. The priory was dissolved in 1537 and the properties granted to the 1st Duke of Suffolk in 1538. Soon afterwards, he sold them to Sir Thomas Pope, from whom James Leveson acquired them in 1540.

4. During the Dissolution of the Monasteries in the reign of Henry VIII, Lilleshall Abbey was surrendered to the Crown and in 1543 purchased by James Leveson. The Leveson family lived in a house adjacent to the Abbey until the outbreak of the English Civil War during which period the Royalists occupied the site until 1645 when, after a long period of resistance, it fell to Cromwell's Parliamentarian troops.

5. One of the four children of the 1st Earl Gower and Mary, his third wife, was the Hon John Leveson-Gower, usually known as the Admiral. Born in 1740, he made the Navy his career. Having joined as a boy, he became a Lieutenant in 1758 and a Captain in 1760 and later a Commodore. In 1787, he became Rear Admiral of the Blue, then the lowest position in the hierarchy of admirals. During this time, Prince William, later King William IV, served as a captain in Leveson-Gower's

squadron. As already noted, an earlier member of the family, Admiral Sir Richard Leveson had fought in the action against the Spanish Armada and, in the Second World War 1939-45), a descendant took part in the naval attack on Zeebrugge.

6. Mary, another daughter of the 1st Earl Gower, was married in 1739 to a baronet, Sir Richard Wrottesley, who was Dean of Worcester from 1765 till his death in 1769. The Wrottesleys were another old Staffordshire landed gentry family.

7. Although Samuel Johnson defined a Gower as a turncoat, he was no less scathing about the Ansons of Shugborough, whom he saw as Whig upstarts - see also the chapter: "Unfortunate Timing".

8. On inheriting the numerous Leveson-Gower estates in 1754, the 2nd Earl Gower soon realised the potential of his lands in Trentham, Lilleshall, Sheriffhales, Donnington Wood, St Georges, Priorslee, Wombridge and Snedshill setting up the Earl Gower & Company business, which eventually became the Lilleshall Company. These companies were involved in many different types of manufacturing activities. In the 20th century, 1,000 acres of this land was sold to the Telford Development Corporation. He also provided some of the loan capital for the Bridgewater Canal and played a leading role in the building of the Trent and Mersey Canal.

9. The 2nd Earl Gower inherited what Disraeli was later to call a talent for 'absorbing heiresses'. His first wife, Elizabeth Fazackerley, was the daughter of rich merchant from Prescot, Lancashire. His second wife, Louisa Egerton, daughter of the 1st Duke of Bridgewater, has already been discussed in the main text of this chapter.

10. Elizabeth Sutherland inherited her father's Earldom following the celebrated *Sutherland Peerage Case,* which established the validity of the unusual practice of this Earldom being able to pass through the female, as well as the male, line. She was an artist, and her work is represented in the Tate Collection.

11. It was on the instructions of Elizabeth, Countess of Sutherland, that her husband (then the Marquis of Stafford) commanded a new Shropshire Seat to be built and the new Lilleshall Hall was completed in 1829. Lilleshall eventually replaced Trentham as the Duke's main English Midlands seat, as the latter was abandoned due to the effects of pollution from the developing Potteries. Trentham Hall was finally demolished in the early 20th century.

12. Francis Egerton, the 3rd and last Duke of Bridgewater, was born on

3 May 1736 and, escaping the scourge of tuberculosis, to which his siblings had succumbed, he carved out for himself a niche in history as the Canal Duke. He had copious reserves of coal under his lands stretching northwards from Worsley, Lancashire, and, furthermore, he had a ready market for that coal in Manchester and Salford, where the demand for fuel simply could not be met. However, the cost of transport from one to the other was prohibitive. The Duke, himself, came up with the solution: a canal, no doubt inspired by the Languedoc Canal in France, which he saw on his Grand Tour of Europe (then a must for young aristocrats) and then spent a lot of time touring its locks and docks. The Languedoc is now known as the Canal du Midi. The Duke was also a subscriber to the Grand Trunk Canal, now more commonly known as the Trent and Mersey Canal.

13. The present Cliveden House, the third on the site, was built by Charles Barry for the 2nd Duke of Sutherland in 1851. Once the home of Nancy, Lady Astor, it is now let as a hotel and is open only on certain days. Although it is a spectacular estate overlooking the River Thames in Buckinghamshire, Cliveden earned a degree of notoriety in the 1960s because of its association with Christine Keeler and Mandy Rice-Davies and the ensuing so-called 'Profumo Affair', which led to the resignation of John Profumo, a Government Minister, and, ultimately, the election of the first Labour Government for 13 years.

14. By 1883, the 3rd Duke of Sutherland was the UK's greatest-ever private landowner with at least 1.4 million acres.

15. Millicent, Duchess of Sutherland, married twice after the death of her husband, the 4th Duke of Sutherland. It was Millicent who attracted the name of 'Meddling Millie' for her activity in supporting women's welfare in the Potteries and the abolition of the use of lead in glazes and paints that caused so much ill health and premature death. In 1898, she also founded a holiday home at Hanchurch for poor Potteries' children and helped found the Potteries & Newcastle Cripples Guild. In Arnold Bennett's book 'The Card', the character 'Interfering Iris, the Countess of Chell' is clearly based on Millie. Arnold Bennett, one of Staffordshire's many famous but often-unsung offspring, is probably better known for such books as 'Anna Of The Five Towns and 'The Old Wives' Tale'. In his novels, the model for 'Sneyd Hall' is said to be Trentham Hall. Sneyd was also the family name of an old landed North Staffordshire family, one of whose homes was Keele Hall now at the centre of Keele University.

16.   The 5th Duke of Sutherland inherited in 1913 at the age of 25 and, with the outbreak of the World War I in the following year, decided that it was unwise to have so much of his capital tied up in land and property. He sold the Trentham Estate and some 250 acres of the Lilleshall Estate retaining the Hall itself and 50 acres of gardens, which were both later sold in 1917.

17.   Francis Egerton (1800-1857), politician, author, and philanthropist changed his name from Leveson-Gower on inheriting the estates of his great uncle, Francis Egerton, 3rd Duke of Bridgewater, when he died in 1803 (See Note 12 above). In Parliament (1822-46), he supported the liberal Tory policies, becoming an early exponent of free trade. He served as Secretary for Ireland (1828-30) and Secretary for War (1830). He supported many intellectual societies, and he enlarged the Bridgewater Collection of paintings and opened it to the public. His many writings include essays, translations, poems, and plays. He was created 1st Earl of Ellesmere in 1846.

A Family Of Influence
Acknowledgements

Cockin, Tim (2000), *The Staffordshire Encyclopaedia,* Malthouse Press; ISBN 0953901807

Gale W K V & Nicholls C R (1979), *The Lilleshall Company: a history 1764-1964,* Moorland Publishing Co Ltd; ISBN 0861900006

Godwin, John (1984), *Some Notable 18th Century Staffordshire M.P.s,* Staffordshire County Council; ISBN 0903363259

Mee, Arthur - ed (1937), *The King's England, Staffordshire,* Hodder & Stoughton

Pevsner, Nicholas (1974), *The Buildings of England, Staffordshire,* Penguin Books Ltd; ISBN 0140710469

Dictionary of National Biography (accessed at Staffordshire County Library)

Elkin, John, *The Leveson-Gower Family,* http://freespace.virgin.net/john.elkin/levgower (accessed 2004)

Lundy, Darryl - compiler, http://www.thepeerage.com/i532.htm#11965 (accessed 2004)

Wikipedia http://en.wikipedia.org/wiki/John_Leveson-Gower,_1st_Earl_Gower et al (accessed 2004)

Wheat, Rose, *Staffordshire Aristocracy* - a course given over six weekends at Wedgwood Memorial College, Winter 1998/9.

Further Reading

Richards, Eric (1973), *The Leviathan of Wealth: Sutherland Fortune in the Industrial Revolution,* Routledge & Kegan Paul; ISBN 070074557

Richards, Eric (1974), *The Industrial Face of a Great Estate: Trentham and Lilleshall (1780-1860),* Economic History Review, Vol 27

Wordie, J R (1982), *Estate Management in Eighteenth-century England - the Building of the Leveson Gower Fortune,* Royal Historical Society Studies in History; ISBN 0901050857

THE LEVESON-GOWERS - SOME FAMILY CONNECTIONS – Page 1

Sir John Leveson (of Haling, Kent, and Lilleshall, Shropshire)
m Frances Sondes, dau of Sir Thomas Sondes

  Frances Leveson
  m Sir Thomas Gower, 2nd Baronet (of Stittenham, Yorkshire)

  3 Sir William Leveson-Gower (4th Baronet)
    m Jean Granville, dau of **John Granville, 1st Earl of Bath**

    A Sir John Leveson-Gower, 1st Lord Gower (Baron)
      m Catherine Manners, dau of **John Manners, 1st Duke of Rutland**

      i John Leveson-Gower, 1st Earl Gower
        m1 Evelyn Pierrepont, dau of **Evelyn Pierrepont, Duke of Kingston**

        c Granville Leveson-Gower, 1st Marquess of Stafford
          m2 Louisa Egerton, dau of **Scrope Egerton, 1st Duke of Bridgewater**

          (1) *George Granville Leveson-Gower, 1st Duke of Sutherland*
            m Elizabeth Gordon, Countess of Sutherland, dau of William Gordon, 18th Earl of Sutherland

            (A) *George Granville Sutherland Leveson-Gower, 2nd Duke of Sutherland*
              m Harriet Elizabeth Georgiana Howard, dau of George Howard, 6th Earl of Carlisle

              (i) *George Granville William Sutherland Leveson-Gower, 3rd Duke of Sutherland*
                m Anne Hay-Mackenzie, Countess of Cromarty

              (b) *Cromartie Sutherland Leveson-Gower, 4th Duke of Sutherland*
                m Millicent Fanny St Clair-Erskine, dau of Robert Francis St Clair-Erskine, 4th Earl of Rosslyn

                ((1)) *Alistair St Claire Sutherland Leveson-Gower, 5th Duke of Sutherland*

        (B) *Francis Leveson-Gower, later Egerton, 1st Earl of Ellesmere*
          m Harriet Catherine Greville

          (i) *George Granville Francis Egerton, 2nd Earl of Ellesmere*
            m Mary Louisa Campbell, dau of 1st Earl of Cawdor

            (a) *Francis Charles Granville Egerton, 3rd Earl of Ellesmere*
              m Catherine Louisa Phipps, dau of George Augustus Constantine Phipps, 2nd Marquess of Normandy

              ((1)) *John Francis Granville Scrope Egerton, 4th Earl of Ellesmere*
                m Violet Lambton, dau of Frederick William Lambton, 4th Earl of Durham

              ((A)) *John Sutherland Egerton, 6th Duke of Sutherland*
                m Diana Evelyn Percy, dau of Alan Ian Percy, 8th Duke of Northumberland

THE LEVESON-GOWERS - SOME FAMILY CONNECTIONS – Page 2

(a) *Francis Charles Granville Egerton, 3rd Earl of Ellesmere (repeated from previous page)*
   m Catherine Louisa Phipps, dau of **George Augustus Constantine Phipps, 2nd Marquess of Normandy**

    ((2)) Francis William George Egerton
       m Hilda Margaret Curteis
       ((B)) Cyril Reginald Egerton
         m Mary Campbell
         ((i)) *Francis Roland Egerton, 7th Duke of Sutherland*
           m Victoria Mary Williams

  (C) Charlotte Sophia Leveson-Gower
    m **Henry Charles Howard, 13th Duke of Norfolk**

  (D) Elizabeth Mary Leveson-Gower
    m **Richard Grosvenor, 2nd Marquess of Westminster**

  (3) Margaret Caroline Leveson-Gower
    m **Frederick Howard, 5th Earl of Carlisle**
  m3 Susannah Stewart, dau of **Alexander Stewart, 6th Earl of Galloway**

  (5) *Granville Leveson-Gower, 1st Earl Granville*

  (6) Georgiana Augusta Leveson-Gower
    m **William Eliot, 2nd Earl of St Germans**

  (7) Charlotte Sophia Leveson-Gower
    m **Henry Charles Somerset, 6th Duke of Beaufort**

  (8) Susan Leveson-Gower
    m **Dudley Ryder, 1st Earl of Harrowby**

  d Gertrude Leveson-Gower
    m **John Russell, 4th Duke of Bedford**

  e Mary Leveson-Gower
    m Sir Richard Wrottesley, Baronet

  g Elizabeth Leveson-Gower
    m **John Waldegrave, 3rd Earl Waldegrave**

  h Evelyn Leveson-Gower
    m2 Richard Vernon of Hilton

The Earl Who Washed His Own Socks

The 5[1] Earl Granville[1], who died in 1996 in his 78th year, spent his later years on the Hebridean island of North Uist. He was a cousin of the Queen through his mother, Lady Rose Constance Bowes-Lyon, an elder sister of Queen Elizabeth, the Queen Mother. He was also regarded as an eccentric old soul whom the Queen would visit on her autumn cruise of the Western Isles - it is said that she once found him washing his socks on a rock by the shore. His son, Granville George Fergus Leveson-Gower, who became the 6th Earl, was Page of Honour to Her Majesty The Queen in 1973/74.

The Granville family name is Leveson-Gower,[2] pronounced 'Looson Gore' and they are kinsmen of the Dukes of Sutherland.

In 1786, Granville Leveson-Gower (1721-1803) was created Marquess of Stafford. He was the son of John Leveson-Gower (d. 1754), who was created Viscount Trentham and Earl Gower in 1746. The public positions held by him included that of Lord Privy Seal, which he filled from 1755 to 1757, and again from 1784 to 1794; of Master of the Horse; of Lord Chamberlain of the Royal Household; and of Lord President of the Council, which he held from 1767 to 1769 and in 1783-1784. The Marquess of Stafford, who was the last survivor of the associates of the Duke of Bedford, commonly known as 'The Bloomsbury Gang', died at Trentham Hall, in Staffordshire, on 26 October 1803. His son and successor, George Granville Leveson-Gower, was created Duke of Sutherland in 1833.

The title of Marquess of Stafford is now borne by the eldest son of the Duke of Sutherland.

Granville Leveson-Gower, a younger son of the 1st Marquess of Stafford, was created Viscount Granville of Stone Park, Co Stafford, in 1815 and Earl Granville [3] on 10 May 1833 in recognition of his services to the country.

As Lord Granville Leveson-Gower, the 1st Earl Granville had entered the diplomatic service and was ambassador at St Petersburg (1804-05 & 1807) and at Paris (1824-28 & 1830-41). [4] He was also a Lord of the Treasury in 1800. He was an intimate friend of George Canning. [5] During his time in Paris, he made a special trip to vote in favour of what became the famous Reform Act of 1832. In this he supported the Whig position for correcting many of the electoral abuses, which had developed over the years. However, this was not the end of electoral reform as will be seen later.

The 2nd Earl Granville was the son of 1st Earl Granville by his wife, Lady Henrietta Elizabeth Cavendish, daughter of the 5th Duke of Devonshire and his wife, Georgiana Spencer.

After entering Parliament in 1836, the 2nd Earl Granville attained high office under a number of Liberal governments. He was Lord President of the Council from 1852 to 1858 and from 1859 to 1866, Secretary of State for the Colonies in 1868 and 1886, Foreign Secretary 1870-4 and 1880-5. He was created a Knight of the Garter in 1857.

The 2nd Earl Granville's name is mainly associated with his career as Foreign Secretary; but the Liberal foreign policy of that period was not distinguished. Although he was known to be a patient and polite person, some historians have claimed that his courteous and pacific methods were somewhat inadequate in dealing with the new situation then arising in Europe and outside it; there is little doubt that foreign governments used the disinclination of the Liberal leaders to take strong measures as an opportunity to stir up trouble for Great Britain.

In Stoke-on-Trent, the 2nd Earl owned the Shelton collieries and was the principal owner of the Etruria Iron Works, as a lessee under the Duchy of Lancaster. His actions in dealing with the miners he employed were somewhat at odds with his actions in the diplomatic world - his decision, in July 1842, at a time of trade depression, to give notice of a reduction of 6d a day in miners' wages, precipitated a miners' strike, which was an element in the background to the Chartist riots of August 1842. [6]

The Earl Who Washed His Own Socks
Further Notes And Connections

1.   For many years, I was a director of the then largest employer in Stone. During that time, a fellow director and I regularly explored Stone over our lunch breaks. On one such occasion, in the 1990s, we discovered that some of the 5th Earl's forebears were buried in a separate corner plot in the grounds of the parish church of St Michael and St Wulfad, Stone. Unfortunately, at that time, the plot had not been tended for some time and was somewhat overgrown - it has since been tidied up. St Michael's churchyard is also the home of the Jervis family mausoleum, in which is interred the body of the most famous member of the family: John Jervis, Earl St Vincent. He took his title from the Battle of Cape St Vincent in 1797. At this battle, Admiral Sir John Jervis, as he was then, led a squadron of 15 against a numerically far superior Spanish fleet. He fell on them off the southern coast of Portugal as they were running for Cadiz and divided their line into two parts. From his flagship, HMS Victory, he ordered his ships to tack in succession and prevent the gap from being closed. Horatio Nelson, last but two in the line, saw that this manoeuvre would not be completed in time and made a quick decision to turn his ship, HMS Captain into the gap. He took on seven Spanish ships, including the Santissima Trinidad, then the largest ship in the world, and two other ships, the San Nicolas and San Josef. Through a hail of pistol and musket fire he led boarding parties onto both and captured both. By nightfall, four ships had been taken and ten others crippled.

2.   The Leveson and Gower families were old established families in Staffordshire and Yorkshire, respectively - see the chapter "A Family Of Influence", which provides more information on these families and their coming together to produce a family, which has probably had more influence on English and British affairs over a longer period of time than any other family in British history other than royalty.

3.   The Granville earldom is one of several, which do not include 'of' in the title, another being the Spencer earldom, the 8th Earl Spencer being better known as the father of the late Diana, the Princess of Wales.

4.   The 1st Earl Granville was an inveterate gambler who was known

amongst the gambling fraternity in Paris as 'le Wellington des jouers'.

5.   George Canning was a Tory Prime Minister for a brief period in 1827. He was the 19th century equivalent of Winston Churchill In oratorical ability, controversy and brilliance. However, his relatively low background aroused distrust in an age of aristocratic politicians. He was a strong supporter of Catholic Emancipation.

6.   Chartism was a British working class movement, which was born during a period of economic depression and named after the People's Charter, drafted by the London Working Men's Association in 1838. The Charter had six demands: universal manhood suffrage; equal electoral districts; voting by ballot; annually elected parliaments; payment of members of parliament; and abolition of property qualifications for members of parliament. Although Chartism collapsed after 1848, most of the Chartist demands were subsequently granted. Chartism was not the first attempt at effecting parliamentary reform in the 19th Century. Earlier attempts had culminated in the Peterloo Massacre in 1819 in Manchester and the Cato Street Conspiracy in 1820. For more background to the events leading up to these two outcomes, refer, respectively, to Sir Charles Wolseley, 7th Baronet, in the chapter: "This Land Was My Land" and to the 1st Earl of Harrowby and the Cato Street Conspiracy in the chapter: "A Near Escape For A Road Builder". In between these early 19th century events and the demise of Chartism came the 1832 Reform Act, which paved the way for the modern parliamentary system.

The Earl Who Washed His Own Socks
Acknowledgements

Gardiner, Juliet ed. (2000), *The History Today Who's Who in British History*, Collins & Brown and CiCo Books; ISBN 1855858827

Godwin, John (1984), *Some Notable 18th Century Staffordshire M.P.s*, Staffordshire County Council; ISBN 0903363259

Elkin, John, *The Leveson-Gower Family*, http://freespace.virgin.net/john.elkin/levgower (accessed 2004)

Wikipedia   http://en.wikipedia.org/wiki/Granville_George_Leveson-Gower%2C_2nd_Earl_Granville (accessed 2004)

Daily Mail

Daily Telegraph

A Near Escape For A Road Builder

Sir Dudley Ryder [1], (1691 - 1756) became a Member of Parliament (MP) and Solicitor-General under Sir Robert Walpole in 1733. In 1737, he was appointed Attorney General and three years later he was knighted. In 1754, he was made Lord Chief Justice of the King's Bench and a Privy Councillor. The patent creating him a peer had just been signed by the king, but not passed, when he died on 25 May 1756. His only son, Nathaniel, who was MP for Tiverton for twenty years, was created Baron Harrowby in 1776.

His eldest son, Dudley Ryder, who was born in London on 22 December 1762, was created the 1st Earl of Harrowby in 1809. He died in 1847. He is the main subject of this piece.

Educated at St John's College, Cambridge, Dudley Ryder became MP for Tiverton in 1784 and under-secretary for foreign affairs in 1789. In 1791, he was appointed Paymaster of the Forces and Vice-President of the Board of Trade, but he resigned the positions and also that of Treasurer of the Navy, when he succeeded to his father's barony in June 1803. In 1804, he was Secretary of State for Foreign Affairs and, in 1805, Chancellor of the Duchy of Lancaster under his intimate friend William Pitt; in the latter year he was sent on a special and important mission to the emperors of Austria and Russia and the king of Prussia, and, for the long period between 1812 and 1827, he was Lord President of the Council.

In February 1820, the Earl of Harrowby had a near escape from a planned assassination attempt, which has gone down in history as the Cato Street Conspiracy. The Cato Street Conspiracy [2] was a plot to blow up the Prime Minister, Lord Liverpool, and the rest of the British Cabinet, when they were thought to be dining at the Earl's house in Grosvenor Square in London. The plotters were a group of radicals led by Arthur Thistlewood, an anti-monarchist former soldier. In fact, a government agent had infiltrated the group and it had been arranged for the plotters to be captured in the room they had taken in Cato Street. [3]

After the death of George Canning [4] in 1827, Lord Harrowby refused to serve George IV as prime minister and he never held office again, although he continued to take part in politics, being especially prominent during the deadlock, which preceded the passing of the Reform Bill in 1832. Harrowby's long association with the Tories did not prevent him from assisting to remove the disabilities of Roman Catholics and Protestant dissenters, or from supporting the movement for electoral reform; he was also in favour of the emancipation of slaves.

Lord Harrowby was also involved in improving the road network in Staffordshire. In the 18th century, turnpike trusts [5,6] carried out improvements throughout the county as in most other counties. Sometimes, they needed Acts of Parliament in order for them to be built. The earl was instrumental in the passing of an act, which helped his estate's business with the workers of the Staffordshire Potteries, who needed provisions to be brought from the countryside.

The earl died at his Staffordshire residence, Sandon Hall, on 26 December 1847.[7] Charles Greville is quoted as saying, "The Earl of Harrowby was the last of his generation and of the colleagues of Mr Pitt, the sole survivor of those stirring times and mighty contests."

The second earl, his eldest son, Dudley Ryder (1798 - 1882), was born in London on 19 May 1798, his mother being Susan, daughter of Granville Leveson-Gower, 1st Marquess of Stafford,[8] and a lady of reputed exceptional attainments. His successor as the third earl was his eldest son, Dudley Francis Stuart Ryder, (1831 - 1900). He died without sons on 26 March 1900, and was succeeded as the 4th earl by his brother, Henry Dudley Ryder (1836 - 1900), whose son, John Herbert Dudley Ryder, became the 5th earl - three earls in the same year!

A Near Escape For A Road Builder
Further Notes and Connections

1. Sir Dudley Ryder was a beneficiary of the 'South Sea Bubble' when he acquired the Digby and Bloxholm estates in Lincolnshire from a Mr Thornton, who was ruined through speculating in the South Sea Scheme.

2. After the end of the French Wars in 1815, it became increasingly clear that England was suffering from great social, economic and political upheavals. These problems collectively became known as the 'Condition of England Question', a description coined in 1839 by Thomas Carlyle, the Scottish essayist and historian. Many of these problems would have occurred eventually but the effects of the French Wars on the country accelerated the process. Most of the major changes were the direct result of the French Wars. Others came from natural growth and change. The distress and discontent caused by these enormous changes were manifested in a series of events in the period 1811-19 including the Spa Field Riots. On 29 January 1820, George III died; this precipitated a constitutional crisis and the calling of a general election. Arthur Thistlewood and his comrades hatched the plot known as the Cato Street Conspiracy early in 1820. Their plan was to overthrow the government and set up a Committee of Public Safety, which would supervise a radical revolution. George Edwards, one of a group of radicals called the Spenceans, suggested that the group should seize the opportunity to kill the entire cabinet during this time of crisis. An advertisement in the newspapers had announced that a 'grand Cabinet dinner' was to be held at the home of the Earl of Harrowby, Lord President of the Council, in Grosvenor Square. This provided an ideal location for the conspirators to do their work.

3. Five of the Cato Street conspirators were sentenced to be transported to Australia as convicts. But the leaders, Arthur Thistlewood and four others, were sentenced to a relatively merciful form of the old high treason punishment of hanging, drawing and quartering - the last people to be so sentenced. In the event, the quartering was not carried out due to a mood change in the watching crowd, which at first jeered the conspirators and then became outraged by events.

4. For a brief note on George Canning, see Note 5 to the chapter: "The Earl Who Washed His Own Socks".

5. Turnpike trusts were set up in the 18th century to introduce a better road network. Before this time, for much of the year, roads were a mass of mud and impassable even for the hardiest traveller. Admiral John Leveson-Gower (of the family referred to in Note 6) is recorded as commenting that he "would rather be in the Bay of Biscay in a storm than on one of the Dilhorne (North Staffordshire) roads in a carriage." Further commentary on transport is given in Appendix 10: The Industrial Revolution and the Development of the Country's Transport Infrastructure. See also Note 5 of the chapter: "A Family Of Influence".

6. Thomas Gilbert, born at Cotton Hall in North Staffordshire, was instrumental in promoting an Act in 1773 consolidating the law relating to turnpikes, which is regarded as a landmark in the history of English highway administration. At the time, he was a Whig Member of Parliament for Lichfield. Thomas trained for a legal career and then served as an ensign with Lord Gower's regiment during the 1745 troubles. After the Battle of Culloden, he began to devote himself to the legal affairs of the Leveson-Gower family - see the chapter: "A Family Of Influence", which is dedicated to the Leveson-Gowers. The 2nd Earl Gower was instrumental in Gilbert becoming a Member of Parliament. Gilbert's main contribution as an MP was his legislation concerning the Poor Law, which he began working on soon after entering Parliament. In 1782, he finally succeeded in passing an act that established 'poor houses' solely for the aged and infirm and introduced a system of outdoor relief for the able-bodied.

7. Sandon Hall, a large and elegant mansion, was destroyed by fire in 1848 and was rebuilt in an even more elegant style.

8. George Granville Leveson-Gower, the 2nd Marquess of Stafford, was created the 1st Duke of Sutherland in 1833. See also the chapters: "A Family of Influence" and "The Earl Who Washed His Own Socks".

A Near Escape For A Road Builder
Acknowledgements

Godwin, John (1984), *Some Notable 18th Century Staffordshire M.P.s*, Staffordshire County Council; ISBN 0903363259

History, Gazetteer and Directory of Staffordshire - William White, Sheffield, 1851

Elkin, John, *The Leveson-Gower Family,* website http://freespace.virgin.net/john.elkin/levgower.... (accessed 2003)

The British Broadcasting Corporation

Here Lies The Leg

Although the 1st Marquess of Anglesey is probably the best known of the Paget family, the Pagets had never been far away from the action in the affairs of England since Tudor times.

Beaudesert Hall [1,2] on Cannock Chase was the Staffordshire home of Henry William Paget, 2nd Earl of Uxbridge and 1st Marquess of Anglesey, who fought with the Duke of Wellington at the Battle of Waterloo.

In 1932, Beaudesert Hall suffered the fate of many other ancestral piles after the First World War - it was demolished. However, the 6th Marquess of Anglesey was not homeless, as he still had Plas Newydd on Anglesey. [3]

By Tudor times, William Paget, [4] who was created 1st Baron Paget de Beaudesert in 1549, was one of the most prominent men of the kingdom. His route to the top had been greatly helped by his father, John Paget, who was said to have been of humble origin, a nail-maker, from Wednesbury, then in Staffordshire but now part of the West Midlands conurbation. John, who had sought his fortune in London, sent William to Trinity Hall, Cambridge. William took full advantage of such a start in life to make some very influential connections, such as with the Boleyn family. These helped him to secure a position in the service of Henry VIII. As well as having good connections, William also proved very adept at skilfully negotiating the minefield of state business and royal whim, which was rather a feat where Henry VIII was concerned.

William Paget acquired large estates from Henry VIII on the dissolution of the monasteries. [5] These estates included Cannock Chase and Burton Abbey [6], both in Staffordshire, as well as West Drayton in Middlesex. Amongst the Staffordshire properties granted to William Paget were the manors of Cannock, Rugeley, Longdon, Beaudesert, Haywood and Abbots Bromley.

On Cannock Chase, he was the first to recognise the area's rich mineral resources. During his time, iron smelting was greatly developed and later family members benefited greatly from the development of coal mining as did other neighbouring aristocracy such as the Littletons.[7,8] On acquiring the Burton-on-Trent properties, William immediately encouraged an expansion of the woollen cloth industry.

William Paget began planning to expand the Manor House, which was within the precincts of Burton Abbey, into a grand mansion. It is not known how much of this ambitious plan was actually carried into effect. Further building work was delayed by William's death in 1563, and the death of his eldest son Henry, the 2nd Baron Paget, a few years later in 1568. However, when the family stayed at the Manor House, they lived in grand style. An inventory of c.1580 shows that there were over 60 rooms, many handsomely furnished.

Before his death, William had become involved in Edward Seymour's plot to become Protector of Edward VI and, following this, he was one of Jane Grey's Privy Councillors, but signed a proclamation in support of Mary shortly afterwards.

William's second son, Thomas, became the 3rd Baron Paget. He concentrated on building Beaudesert House, which became the Paget family's main residence and would remain in the family until the 20th century. However, he was a zealous Roman Catholic and became involved in the Throckmorton Plot to overthrow Elizabeth I and place Mary, Queen of Scots, on the throne. As a result, he was attainted in 1587 - the family estates were forfeited and the title lost. He died around 1589/1590. It is likely that Thomas became embroiled in such plots through his youngest brother, Charles, who was a well-known Catholic conspirator, although, at times, he also played the part of a spy and forwarded information to Sir Francis Walsingham, Elizabeth's spymaster, and William Cecil, 1st Lord Burghley.

William, 4th Baron Paget (1572 - 1629), who had become a Protestant, was restored to his estates and to his title by James I around 1604. In 1612, he became a member of the Virginia Company, which then included Bermuda. He was one of the 'Adventurers' who invested in the Bermuda Company to colonise the Bermuda islands from 1615 onwards.

His son, William, the 5th Lord Paget (1609 - 1678), fought for Charles I at Edgehill.

William, the 6th Lord (1637 - 1713), a supporter of the Revolution of 1688, was ambassador at Vienna from 1689 to 1693, when he moved to Constantinople on his appointment as Ambassador Extraordinary to Turkey. In this role he participated in the negotiations for a treaty of peace between the Imperialists, Poles and Turks, resulting in the Treaty of Carlowitz on 26 January 1699.

William was also involved in opening up navigation on the River Trent, which enabled Burton-upon-Trent to become an inland port with access to the Baltic trade via the North Sea during the 17th and 18th centuries.[9]

Henry, the 7th Baron (c. 1665 - 1743), was raised to the peerage during his father's lifetime as Baron Burton in 1712, being one of the twelve peers created by the Tory ministry to secure a majority in the House of Lords, and was created Earl of Uxbridge in 1714. His only son, Thomas Catesby Paget, the author of an Essay on Human Life and other writings, died in January 1742 before his father, leaving a son Henry (1719 - 1769), who became 2nd Earl of Uxbridge. At the latter's death, the earldom of Uxbridge and barony of Burton became extinct. However, the older barony of Paget of Beaudesert passed to his cousin, Henry Bayley (1744 - 1812), heir general of the first baron, who benefited from the apparent prescience of the 1st Baron in managing to arrange for his peerage to be transmittable through the female line in the event of the male line dying out. Henry Bayley's mother was Caroline Paget, a cousin of the 8th Baron.

Henry Bayley assumed the name and arms of Paget by royal licence on 29 January 1770 and on 19 May 1784 was created Earl of Uxbridge (second creation). His second son, Sir Arthur Paget (1771 - 1840), was an eminent diplomat during the Napoleonic wars and Sir Edward Paget (1775 - 1849), the fourth son, served under Sir John Moore in the Peninsular War (1809 - 1813), and was afterwards second in command under Sir Arthur Wellesley, 1st Duke of Wellington; the fifth son, Sir Charles Paget (1778 - 1839), served with distinction in the navy, and rose to the rank of vice-admiral. Henry's eldest son Henry William, 2nd Earl of Uxbridge (1768 - 1854), is now best known as the 1st Marquess of Anglesey (created in 1815 after the Battle of Waterloo).

The 1st Marquess began his career in the infantry but entered the cavalry. The 7th light dragoons (later the 7th Hussars) were under his command and he developed them into one of the best cavalry units in the army. He commanded the cavalry in the Peninsula War under Moore but was not used by Wellington despite his experience. Unfortunately, in 1809, he had eloped with Wellington's sister-in-law, the wife of his brother Henry and then already a mother of four. Despite their marriage after his divorce, Henry Paget saw no further service in Portugal or Spain due to social restrictions and the code of honour of this time, although Wellington himself did not mind commenting "He will not run away with me!". This incident had followed the La Corunna campaign of 1808-09 and, as a result, the British cavalry in the Peninsula was deprived of the only real cavalry commander the British Army possessed. Nevertheless, old differences were settled by the divorce and subsequent remarriage.[10] Paget commanded the cavalry and horse artillery at Waterloo with distinction. But he lost a leg doing so, which prevented his further military service. This amputated leg has since become something of a legendary object.

The inscription on the memorial at Waterloo reads "Here lies the leg of his Majesty's illustrious, brave and valiant Lieutenant-General the Earl of Uxbridge commander-in-chief of the English, Belgian and Dutch cavalry wounded on the 18th of June at the memorable battle of Waterloo who by his heroism contributed to the triumph of mankind's cause so gloriously decided by the brilliant victory of that day." [11,12] It is now known that the leg no longer lies here but its eventual fate is another interesting story in its own right. [13]

In 1818, the Marquess of Anglesey was made a knight of the Garter and, at the coronation of George IV he acted as Lord High Steward of England.[14] For a time, his support of the proceedings against Queen Caroline made him unpopular, and when, on one occasion, he was beset by a crowd, who compelled him to shout " The Queen," he is reported as adding the wish, " May all your wives be like her."

The Marquess had a large family by each of his two wives: two sons and six daughters by the first, Caroline Elizabeth Villiers, and six sons and four daughters by the second, Charlotte Cadogan. His eldest son, Henry, succeeded him; but the title passed rapidly in succession to the 3rd, 4th and 5th Marquesses. The latter, whose extravagances were notorious, died in 1905, when the title passed to his cousin. [15]

Here Lies The Leg
Further Notes and Connections

1. The spelling 'Beaudesert' was in use in 1293 but has been variously spelt since.

2. It has been said that Sir Walter Scott refers to Beaudesert in the 'Lady of the Lake' - canto 6.

3. Other Staffordshire houses, which also suffered the fate of demolition, include Tixall Hall (c 1926), Teddesley Hall (1954) and Wolseley Hall (1965). For details of further houses demolished, see Appendix 3: The Demise of the English Country House.

4. William Paget (1506 - 1563) was educated at St Paul's School, Trinity Hall, Cambridge, and the University of Paris. During Henry VIII's reign, he became a Privy Councillor, Secretary of State, Comptroller of the King's Household, Chancellor of the Duchy of Lancaster and a Knight of the Garter.

5. See Appendix 7: Dissolution of the Monasteries and The Reformation for more background on these socio-religious events.

6. The Paget family remained important landowners around Burton-on-Trent until 1919 when most of the property belonging to the Marquess of Anglesey was sold off.

7. In 1560, William Paget and his son and heir, Henry, were given licence to fell trees on Cannock Chase and elsewhere in the county for fuel in the making of iron using ironstone from Walsall. He had two iron mills at work on the Chase when he died in 1563. It has also been claimed that one of these was the first blast furnace in the Midlands. In the 17th century, another well-known Staffordshire family, the Chetwynds, forebears of the later Earls of Shrewsbury, became involved in these iron works - see also the chapter: "The Premier Earls" for more on the Earls of Shrewsbury.

8. See the chapter: "How To Be Comfortable In Church" for more details on the Littleton family.

9. William, the 6th Lord Paget, and his agents had reacted favourably to pressure from the Burton-upon-Trent inhabitants to open up navigation between Burton and Wilden and, on 4 May 1699, an Act of Parliament was passed authorising Lord Paget to construct 'such Locks, Wears,

Turnpikes, Pens for Water, Cranes, Wharfs, Warehouses and other things proper and convenient' between Burton and Wilden Ferry in Derbyshire. However, little seems to have happened and a further attempt in 1714 to improve matters also appears to have failed. More progress was made following the opening of the Grand Trunk Canal (later known as the Trent and Mersey Canal) in 1777.

10. At the time of Henry Paget's elopement with Lady Charlotte Wellesley, he was married to Lady Caroline Villiers and was a father of eight children. At the time, Lady Caroline received most of the sympathy but it was later revealed that she had had a long-standing affair with the Duke of Argyll. Although both divorces were messy, there was a neat ending - Henry married Lady Charlotte and Lady Caroline married her Duke.

11. The Battle of Waterloo did not really take place in Waterloo, but further south. Wellington always named his battles after the places he stayed at, not where they were fought.

12. The Wellington Museum in Waterloo contains a very clear presentation on the battle, and includes examples of uniforms, weapons, and furniture. You can see the wooden leg of Lord Uxbridge, later to be the 1st Marquess of Anglesey. Lord Uxbridge was Wellington's second in command. As they rode together during the battle, a cannonball struck him in the leg. It is reputed that he turned to Wellington and said, "By God, sir, I've lost my leg" to which Wellington replied, "By God, sir, so you have."

13. On Saturday, 31 January 2004, BBC Radio 4 broadcast a light-hearted but interesting programme, presented by Neil Mullarkey, called 'The Curious Life Of Lord Uxbridge's Leg', in which he set out to trace the last resting place of this famous appendage. His search started at Lichfield Cathedral, where the first Marquess of Anglesey is buried along with several of his Paget forebears in the Paget Vaults. His journey ended in Belgium with the disappointing but rather poignant discovery that the remaining bones had come to an ignominious end in 1934 following the death of Louis Paris, a descendant of Hyacinthe Paris, who had originally buried the leg. Whilst clearing his effects, Louis Paris's widow found the bones in his private collection. Horrified, she ordered her servants to burn the bones in the boiler of the central heating system. So ended over two hundred years of separate existence for Lord Uxbridge's leg. But this is not quite the end of the story for even his replacement artificial legs received fame - one of the first

types is still preserved at Plas Newydd, the family home on Anglesey and the new type of artificial limb invented by Potts was named the 'Anglesey Leg'. The general design remained in use up to the early part of the 20th century.

14.   See Appendix 6: Great Offices of State of England for a summary of these offices, which are now mainly of a ceremonial nature.

15.   Henry Cyril Paget, 5th Marquess of Anglesey, died bankrupt in Monte Carlo in 1905. He was aged just 29. His life had been devoted to the unbridled and unashamed squandering of a very large private fortune. He spent everything on the creation of his own opulent world, driven by an obsessional pursuit of aesthetic fulfilment. He was an extremely flamboyant extrovert; his principal interests were dressing up, collecting and wearing very expensive jewellery, dancing and staging lavish theatrical extravaganzas. His nickname was 'The Dancing Marquess', and was probably used less than affectionately by the rest of his family. He was born in 1875 and brought up in France, largely in the company of theatrical people. These formative years clearly instilled a deep love of showing off, and, upon entering the family seat at Plas Newydd, his first act was to convert the centuries old chapel into a theatre. From 1901 onwards, he staged a series of productions whose scale and cost were boundless. Casts of 50 or 60 were clad in luxurious, fantastic costumes and large amounts of jewellery. Paget was especially fond of 'Aladdin', and it is believed this light opera was the most performed work by his company. He played the part of Pekoe, and during the interval would perform his celebrated 'Butterfly Dance'. What this actually consisted of is unclear, although large gossamer-effect wings and huge clusters of colourful jewels, and a great deal of running around with arms flapping can be guessed at. Hence 'The Dancing Marquess'. In just four years, Paget spent his entire fortune on luxurious goods, clothes, jewels and the upkeep of very large casts of actors for his productions, which would tour Britain and the Continent. It is not known how much he actually spent, but the jewellery alone for his own Henry V costume cost £40,000, equivalent to over £4,000,000 by the end of the 20th century. That was just one costume out of hundreds made for his company over the years. Sadly, very little information about Henry Cyril Paget exists today. After his death, he was succeeded by his cousin, the 6th Marquess of Anglesey, whose first priority was to reconvert the chapel and systematically destroy all evidence that Henry Cyril Paget had ever existed. Luckily,

for future generations of visitors to Plas Newydd, Anglesey, there are now some references to Henry Cyril Paget around the house.

Here Lies The Leg
Acknowledgements

Owen, C C (1978), *The Development of Industry in Burton-upon-Trent*, Phillimore & Co; ISBN 0850332184

Godwin, J (1992), *Beaudesert, The Pagets and Waterloo*, J Godwin; ISBN 0951591320

Stone, Richard (2002), *A Stone's Throw of Burton*, RS Enterprises; ISBN 0953652718

The Victoria History of the County of Stafford - extracts

The British Broadcasting Corporation (BBC) – 'The Curious Life of Lord Uxbridge's Leg', Neil Mullarkey, BBC Radio 4, 31 January 2004

History of Beaudesert Park - Bernard Richards

www.beaudesert.org/history/beau_book.htm (accessed 2004)

The Idler website http://www.idler.co.uk/ (accessed 2004)

How To Be Comfortable In Church

Penkridge is a small Staffordshire town, which lies on the A449 between Stafford and Wolverhampton.

The Tudor period saw the local struggle for power around Penkridge between the Dudleys of Warwick and the Littletons of Pillaton, a small settlement close to Penkridge. Although both families were already wealthy, they both became even richer from the acquisition of Church lands confiscated during the Dissolution of the Monasteries.[1] Following the Reformation, the Collegium at Penkridge was dissolved and stone from its building used to build some of the houses in the village. It is still possible to see examples of this stone in the bases of some of the village's buildings.

One of the early family members, Sir Thomas Littleton, bought the Tixall Manor [2] from Rose Merston (née de Wasteney) in 1469.

In 1529, Sir Edward Littleton succeeded to the lands of Huntington, Teddesley, Pillaton and Otherton held by his mother, Alice, heiress of William de Wynnesbury, and wife of Richard Littleton. In 1544, Wolgarston was bought from the four daughters of William Hussey, who had died in 1532 [3]; Levedale and Longridge from the Wingfields in 1542; the Deanery Manor was acquired on an 80 year lease in 1543 and parts of Acton - Bednall estates were bought from Elizabeth de Vere [4], wife of John de Vere, 15th Earl of Oxford, in 1541 and 1547.

In 1575, Elizabeth I was a guest at the White Hart, which, at that time, was the manor house of Ambrose Dudley, Earl of Warwick.[5]

It was Sir Edward Littleton (1727 - 1812), Member of Parliament for Staffordshire (1784 - 1812), who chose the site for the new Hall at Teddesley. In 1742, Sir Edward had succeeded to the estates and baronetcy of the 3rd baronet, his uncle (also called Sir Edward) of Pillaton Hall.[5] However, the new baronet was encouraged to look for a new seat, as Pillaton Hall occupied a low site and was not in good condition. By 1745, Sir Edward had moved into Teddesley Hall, which remained the main seat of the Littleton family until 1930 when the 3rd Lord Hatherton died. The 4th Lord Hatherton then moved the family seat from Teddesley to Hatherton. Teddesley was eventually demolished in 1954.[6]

When Sir Edward Littleton, 4th Baronet, succeeded in 1742, he inherited 6,524 acres and added a further 1,911 acres between 1749 and 1809 by buying out smaller freeholders around Penkridge. The Littleton family continued to be large landowners in Staffordshire, especially around Penkridge, into the twentieth century.[7,8]

Sir Edward was also an early supporter of the development of the canal system in England. He became a large shareholder in the Staffordshire and Worcestershire Canal Company and gave permission for the Canal to pass for about four miles through his estates.[9]

In the early part of the 19th century, at the local parish church of St Michael's in Penkridge, Lord Hatherton, the head of the Littleton family, had the pews for his family taken out and replaced with armchairs and a working fireplace.[10] When he thought the sermon had gone on long enough he would rattle the pages of 'The Times' to indicate that it was time to finish.

Edward John Walhouse Littleton [11] (created the first Baron Hatherton in 1835) was the British government's Chief Secretary for Ireland in 1833 - 34. In 1834, he opened secret negotiations with Daniel O'Connell, an Irish member of parliament, who was one of the leading campaigners against the Act of Union.[12]

Many famous people knew and visited Penkridge through their visits to Teddesley Hall. They included the Duke of Wellington, Sir Robert Peel, George Frederick Handel, John Wesley, Alexis de Tocqueville [13], Daniel Defoe[14] and George Orwell. On visiting the annual horsefair in 1724, Daniel Defoe is quoted as having said, "In a word I believe I may mark it the greatest horsefair in the world for horses of value".

By the latter part of the 19th century, coal was playing an important role in mid-Staffordshire. The Littleton Colliery had its first shaft sunk in 1877 by the Cannock and Huntington Colliery Company, but ran into serious problems with water and was abandoned for sixteen years after collapsing around 1881. However, in 1897, Lord Hatherton reopened the site and sank a new shaft and, by 1899, the Littleton Colliery had been established.[15] By 1954, this colliery was the largest in the Cannock coalfield and was worked until the mid 1990's.

How To Be Comfortable In Church
Further Notes and Connections

1.   In 1546, Sir William Paget (see the chapter: "Here Lies The Leg") was granted most of the Church lands in the Cannock Chase area belonging to the Cathedral of Lichfield and the Abbey of Burton. Among these properties were the manors of Pillaton and Whiston, both of which were leased to the existing occupiers - the Littletons and the Giffards. For more on the Dissolution of the Monasteries and the Reformation see the Appendix of the same name.

2.   Tixall Manor remained in the Littleton family until 1507 when Joan Littleton married Sir John Aston of Haywood - see the chapter: "What's In A Family Name" for more on the Astons, one of the last in line, Barbara, marrying into the Clifford family.

3.   The Husseys had held property in the Penkridge area since at least the 12th century when Walter Hussey held Penkridge Manor.

4.   Elizabeth de Vere, née Trussell, Countess of Oxford, was the daughter of Edward Trussell, who had held Acton Trussell since 1480.

5.   Ambrose Dudley, who was created the Earl of Warwick in 1564, was the son of John Dudley, 1st Duke of Northumberland, and a brother of Robert Dudley, who was created the Earl of Leicester, also in 1564. Robert is best known as one of Queen Elizabeth 1's favourites. John Dudley was executed for his role in attempting to place Lady Jane Grey on the throne – Jane was married to Guildford Dudley, another of his sons. The Earldom of Leicester became extinct on Robert Dudley's death in 1588. However, his nephew, Robert Sidney, who had inherited his property, was created Earl of Leicester in 1618. Robert Sidney died in 1626 at Penshurst, his country seat. Penshurst had originally been one of the properties of the Stafford family but was forfeited after the execution of Edward Stafford, 3rd Duke of Buckingham in 1521 – see the chapter: "Titles Move In Mysterious Ways".

6.   It is reputed that the cost of building Teddesley Hall was largely covered by the discovery of hoards of coins found behind the panelling at Pillaton Hall.

7.   The 5th Lord Hatherton, who succeeded in 1944, had found himself the victim of heavy death duties. In addition, Teddesley Hall had suffered

much damage after being requisitioned by the government for military purposes during the Second World War. He had sold it to a local farmer just 18 months before and he decided to retain detached buildings on either side of the main hall for the storage of agricultural produce. John Harris in his book 'No Voice from the Hall' writes, "I found on its grassy plateau just two grand baroque brick stable ranges with strong rusticated stone windows. They surveyed the landscape with no purpose, the formal outlines of the garden long since erased". See also Appendix 3: The Demise of the English Country House.

8.   The great Liberal victory in 1906 ushered in a period of social reform, necessitating higher taxation. For several years, the 3rd Lord Hatherton continued as usual in spite of a declining income. However, in 1919, the now ageing Lord Hatherton sold over 360 acres of the Deanery Manor (first acquired on lease in 1543 - see 1 above); 250 acres, including the Spread Eagle at Gailey; 500 acres at Levedale; 340 acres at Longridge and two farms - Preston Vale and Preston Hill.

9.   As noted in the main text, Sir Edward Littleton (1727-1812) had played an important part in the development of the canal system around Penkridge. The act of parliament to construct the canal was passed in 1766 and James Brindley, the famous canal engineer, was appointed to build the canal between the river Severn in Worcestershire and the Trent and Mersey Canal at Great Haywood in Staffordshire. By 1772, the 46 miles long canal, with its 43 locks, had been completed. The northern end of the canal skirts the extensive parkland of Shugborough Hall, home to the Anson family - Earls of Lichfield, before entering the Tixall Wide. Here the canal was widened out to satisfy the demands of Thomas Clifford, from Tixall Hall, who wanted the canal to take on the appearance of an ornamental lake to form part of his landscaped grounds - see also the chapter: "What's In A Family Name" for more on the Cliffords (and Astons) of Tixall.

10.   Imperial Vanities - see Acknowledgements below.

11.   In 1812, Sir Edward Littleton, 4th Baronet, died, leaving no male heir in the direct line, and the baronetcy became extinct. The Littleton estates passed to Edward John Walhouse, grandson of Moreton Walhouse of Hatherton, who had married Sir Edward's sister, Frances Littleton. In accordance with the terms of his great-uncle's will, Walhouse now assumed the surname and arms of Littleton. Mary, his wife, was the daughter of Richard Wellesley, brother of the Duke of Wellington, the Iron Duke. The wife of Henry Wellesley, another brother of the Iron

Duke, eloped with the future 1st Marquess of Anglesey – for more on this, see the chapter: "Here Lies The Leg".

12. Lord Althorp (a forebear of Diana, Princess of Wales) sanctioned Littleton's proposal to see Daniel O'Connell in June 1834 in order to find out what the Irish members really wanted, and authorised him to say, as was the fact, that the clauses in the Coercion Bill prohibiting public meetings were still under discussion, but not to commit the government and himself. He had afterwards to bear his share of the blame when O'Connell broke the pledge of secrecy under which the interview took place. Personally, he was opposed to the prohibition of public meetings, but had been overruled by the majority of his colleagues, though he carried his opposition to the verge of resignation; but when O'Connell declared on 3 July in the House of Commons that Littleton, in order to gain time to carry a by-election at Wexford, had given him Althorp's assurance that the prohibition of the meetings was to be abandoned, both he and the ministry were made to appear either to have played O'Connell false or to have introduced a bill which ran counter to their convictions. In fact no such assurance had been authorised, or perhaps in any such form given, and Littleton had kept to himself the fact that he had given any assurance at all. On 7 July, Althorp spoke in defence of Littleton, and cleared him from the charge of having duped O'Connell; but when the opposition threatened to move for correspondence between the Irish and the home government, he tendered his resignation to Lord Grey. As he was indispensable to the ministry, Lord Grey resigned too, on 9 July. Grey's place was taken by Lord Melbourne. But on 11 July, 206 Liberal members sent Althorp an address deprecating his retirement. Althorp's personal wish was that the king should send for Peel. However, following an urgent request from Melbourne and Grey, he consented to refer the question of his return to office to his three friends, Lord Ebrington, Lord Tavistock, and Mr. Bonham Carter. Their decision was that, on the understanding that the ministry would drop 'the meeting clauses' from the new Coercion Bill, he should resume office, and, after adding a stipulation that Littleton should be reinstated also, Althorp acquiesced.

13. Alexis de Tocqueville was a French philosopher and author, whose most famous work is 'Democracy in America' written after visits to the fledgling United States and England to study the forms of government. The first part of the book was published in 1835. Tocqueville's theories still remain popular. One reason is because he appeals to all sides of

the political and social spectrum. One does not have to be a liberal or conservative to appreciate Tocqueville's theories. Politicians often quote Tocqueville because it is 'in' to do so. Tocqueville's theories of crime and punishment remain popular because they are based on the timeless principles of equality, liberty and justice. While these principles may be somewhat vague and idealistic, they remain ingrained in the American perception of crime and justice. As a result, Tocqueville will probably remain popular for many years to come.

14. Daniel Defoe (1660-1731) is probably best known for his novels 'Robinson Crusoe' and 'Moll Flanders'. He is also considered to be the founder of British journalism. He started his literary career as a poet. He also wrote a three volume travel book 'Tour Through the Whole Island of Great Britain' (1724-27), which provided a first hand account of the state of the country at that time.

15. Coal-loading facilities were erected on the canal south of Otherton and Penkridge became an inland coal-port. Coal-laden barges sailed down the Staffordshire and Worcestershire Canal as far as Stourport, and, by means of the Shropshire Union Canal, to Shrewsbury and then via its Welsh branches, as far as Welshpool and Llangollen.

How To Be Comfortable In Church
Acknowledgements

Andrews, Anne (1995), *A History of Tixall - 1. Tixall's Churches,* Hanyards Press; ISBN 0952742519

Godwin, John (1984), *Some Notable 18th Century Staffordshire M.P.s,* Staffordshire County Council; ISBN 0903363259

Harris, John (1998), *No Voice from the Hall: Early Memories of a Country House Snooper,* John Murray; ISBN 0719555671

Thompson, Brian (2001), *Imperial Vanities,* HarperCollins; ISBN 0002571889

Wilkes, Robert Charles (1985), *The Story of Penkridge,* Penkridge Parish Council; ISBN 0951094203

History, Gazetteer and Directory of Staffordshire - William White, Sheffield, 1851

bz.llano.net/gowen/hussey_millenium/husseyms_001.htm

Robert Maddocks' article http://www.penkridge.org.uk/history.htm (accessed 2004)

Spartacus Educational website http://www.spartacus.schoolnet.co.uk/PRpeel.htm (accessed 2004)

How To Get Rid Of Your Relatives

The Harpur (later Harpur-Crewe) family lived at Calke in Derbyshire from the reign of James I until the early 20th Century. By clever marriages, they were able to build up their wealth, which enabled Sir John Harpur to build Calke Abbey in the early 18th Century. Calke Abbey has been described as one of the more tantalisingly inaccessible houses in England along with Narford Hall, Norfolk, and Shirburn Castle, Oxfordshire. To these names, I would add Trelowarren in Cornwall, the former home of the Vyvyan family.

Calke Abbey stands on the site of a religious house, Calke Priory, which was closed during the Dissolution of the Monasteries ordered by Henry VIII.[1] The Calke Abbey name was only adopted in the 19th century.

The Calke estate was purchased in 1622 for Henry Harpur, who purchased a baronetcy in 1626. However, the Harpur family had already been well established in that area of Derbyshire since the mid 1500s, through Sir Henry's grandfather, Richard Harpur, who married an heiress, Jane Findern. Eventually, Jane inherited land in Findern, Swarkestone, Repton, Ticknall, Twyford, Stanton-by-Bridge and elsewhere in south Derbyshire.

Richard's son, John, was deeply involved in local affairs as a Justice of the Peace and a right-hand man of the Earls of Shrewsbury,[2] who were then leading magnates in Derbyshire, Staffordshire and elsewhere. John Harpur acquired the manor of Warslow, Staffordshire, in 1593. At that time, John was already described as the lord of Alstonefield, another nearby Staffordshire settlement.

Later Harpurs developed marked signs of oddness and one descendant, Sir Henry Harpur, upset social convention by his marriage to a lady's maid, and, by cutting himself off from society, became known in his lifetime as 'the isolated baronet'. In 1808, he changed his name to Crewe in a vain attempt to improve his chances of reviving the dormant barony of Crewe of Steane.

His reclusive nature re-emerged in his great grandson, Sir Vauncy Harpur-Crewe, who was descended from him through both parents. In Sir Vauncey could be found all the marked characteristics of the family: reclusiveness, a passion for collecting and an equally absorbing fascination with natural history.

When his grandson, Mr Henry Harpur-Crewe,[3] handed over the house to the National Trust in 1985, Calke was virtually as Sir Vauncey had left it at his death in 1924. In fact, in many ways, it was almost unchanged from when he had inherited in 1886. The Harpur-Crewes were a family who threw nothing away but simply filled rooms with their 'treasures' until they were full then shut the doors and moved on to the next room to fill. In fact, one uninspired National Trust assessor was reported as describing the contents as "twenty skipsful of junk".

Sir Vauncey has to have a leading place in the gallery of great British eccentrics. Having abdicated his social responsibilities, he devoted himself almost entirely to the pursuit of birds and butterflies accompanied by his head gamekeeper, Agathos Pegg, his only confidant. He treated the park at Calke as a private bird sanctuary and forbade his agricultural tenants to trim their hedges in order to provide cover for nesting birds. Nonetheless, this did not stop him from shooting and stuffing them before filling the house with the creatures.

Little seen outside the bounds of Calke and his secondary seat in Warslow over the border in Staffordshire [4], Sir Vauncey was regarded as a benevolent despot, combining great solicitude for his tenants and employees with a degree of aloofness and disdain towards his own family. An example of this was an altercation he had with a cousin on the lawn of Repton Park, another house on the Calke estate, whilst out on one of his hunting expeditions. On his return to Calke afterwards, the outraged baronet sent for his agent and gave orders for Repton to be demolished. Within a week, the offending house had been pulled down and the wretched cousin was obliged to find a new home.

His relationships with his own children were sometimes so strained that he would communicate with them only by letter, delivered by a footman on a silver salver or, even sometimes, through the public post! His daughter, Airmyne,[5] was the only one of his four daughters to obey his edict not to marry but even she was turned out of the house when he caught her breaking the ban on smoking, which he had imposed on all his household for fear of fire. She never returned during his lifetime.

He also banned motor cars and bicycles from the grounds. Visitors had to park at the gates and were then collected by carriage.

After the death of Sir Vauncey's daughter, Hilda Mosley, in 1949, the family sold most of the farmland on the Alstonefield estate in 1951 to pay death duties. In 1986, the moorland was transferred to the Peak Park joint planning board in lieu of capital transfer tax.

Although the death in 1999 of Airmyne's niece, also called Airmyne, brought the family line to an end, the family has managed to leave its mark, hopefully for posterity, in its archives – the entire Harpur-Crewe collection of over 500 boxes containing masses of documents, including a Royal decree from 1565 granting the family the use of a crest, letters, manuscripts maps and deeds. So typical of the family, many of these papers were found in attics and outbuildings. The Harpur-Crewe collection is now held in Derbyshire County Council's Record Office, New Street, Matlock. Some of the records go back to the 12th Century.

How To Get Rid Of Your Relatives
Further Notes and Connections

1. Calke Priory was an Augustinian house, which owed its foundation to Richard, 2nd Earl of Chester, who had inherited vast estates in England and Normandy. The foundation was sometime between 1115 and 1120, the latter year being when Richard died, a victim of the White Ship disaster, in which Henry I's son and heir together with many courtiers also died when the ship was lost crossing from Normandy to England. Ranulph, the 6th Earl of Chester, founded Dieulacres Abbey, near Leek in Staffordshire - see the chapter: "The North Staffordshire Wallabies". See also Appendix 7: Dissolution of the Monasteries and the Reformation.

2. For more information on the Earls of Shrewsbury, see the chapter: "The Premier Earls".

3. Henry Harpur-Crewe was the younger son of Sir Vauncey's youngest daughter, Frances, who married Arthur William Jenney. Henry was born in 1921, changed his name to Harpur-Crewe in 1961 and died in 1991. Henry had two siblings - Charles and Airmyne (see note 5 below). Henry also showed signs of inheriting the Harpur-Crewe eccentricity traits as illustrated in a strange encounter reported by Rupert Gunnis, an antiquarian. One Sunday morning at Calke he found the gateway was locked to the churchyard in the park; he then witnessed the arrival of the priest and a line of tenants, more old than young, each bending down to crawl through a hole in the fence because Henry (then Jenney) refused to unlock the churchyard gate.

4. At one time, the Harpur estates amounted to almost 34,000 acres - 20,000 in Staffordshire (around Warslow and Alstonefield), 13,000 in Derbyshire and 877 acres in Leicestershire.

5. Sir Richard FitzHerbert of Tissington Hall wrote the following about the death in 1999 of Henry Harpur-Crewe's sister, also called Airmyne: "The recent death of Miss Airmyne Harpur-Crewe of Warslow and Calke Abbey has seen the end of an era in Derbyshire families. Aged 80, Miss Airmyne died in April having been the last descendant of that famous eccentric family of Ticknall."

How To Get Rid Of Your Relatives
Acknowledgements

Colvin, H M (1996), *Calke Abbey*, The National Trust; ISBN 0707800994; 1996

Harris, John (1998), *No Voice From The Hall: Early Memories of a Country House Snooper*, John Murray; ISBN 0719555671

Unfortunate Timing

Compared with other Staffordshire landowners, the Anson family are relative newcomers as far as Shugborough is concerned - William Anson, a successful barrister, purchased the Shugborough property, which consisted of a mediaeval manor house standing in only 80 acres of land, in 1624.[1] In 1695, his grandson, also named William, began building the new house and acquiring additional land. Following William's death in 1720, his son, Thomas, further extended the house, and continued to expand the estate. By 1741, Thomas owned almost a quarter of the village. In 1762, Thomas inherited the estate of his childless brother, George Anson, better known as Admiral Lord Anson.[2,3] When Thomas died in 1773, the Anson family controlled virtually the whole of Shugborough, plus a vast area of Cannock Chase.[4,5]

Thomas was a bachelor and, on his death, the Anson line came to an end. The estate passed to his sister's son, George Adams of Orgreave, near Lichfield. George took the name Anson and his son, Thomas, was created the 1st Viscount Anson.

From 1795 onwards, Viscount Anson totally remodelled the Shugborough estate with the intention of adapting a purely ornamental landscape to the needs of farming in the great age of agricultural improvement. To many people, the name of Staffordshire is closely linked to the development of industry - The Potteries in the north of the county and the Black Country in the south of the county. However, in the late 18th century, Staffordshire was as much in the vanguard of agricultural development and Viscount Anson had every intention of being right at the front - the Park Farm at Shugborough was intended to exceed all others in the county in scale and in the excellence of its buildings.[6]

The 1st Viscount also purchased the Ranton Abbey Estate, which was greatly expanded by his son, Thomas William, who was created the 1st Earl of Lichfield in 1831 in the Coronation Honours of William IV. The 1st Earl bought more land, planting coverts and spending large sums of money in making it one of the finest sporting estates in the country. However, his spending exceeded his income substantially [7] and, in 1838, all his debts were consolidated into a single large mortgage of £600,000. In 1842, this was followed by the sale of the contents of both his London house and Shugborough. Following the sale,

Shugborough was shut up, the home farm was let to a tenant farmer and Lord and Lady Lichfield went to live abroad until 1847. On their return, they lived quietly, more often at Ranton than Shugborough, until Lord Lichfield's death in 1854. He was succeeded by his son, Thomas George, who, in the following year, married Harriet Georgina Louisa Hamilton, the eldest daughter of the 2nd Marquess of Abercorn, who was later created the 1st Duke of Abercorn in 1868.[8,9]

The large mortgage of £600,000 taken out in 1838 had been manageable for around 30 years until the agricultural depression of the 1870s, which resulted in a dramatic fall in estate revenues making it more difficult to meet interest payments.[10] However, Shugborough was saved by the 2nd Earl's son, Thomas Francis, who took over the management of the estate in 1880. Thomas Francis became the 3rd Earl of Lichfield in 1892. Like many late 19th century landowners, he made up for the decline in agricultural rents by diversifying into other activities such as investing in the colonies and taking on City directorships. By good financial management, he was able to reduce substantially the mortgages on the estate. In addition, he sold off many of the burgages bought in the mid-18th century before later parliamentary reforms made them ineffective as a means of helping to secure a parliamentary seat.

The 3rd Earl died in 1918 from an accident whilst out shooting. He was succeeded by his son, Thomas Edward, who married first Evelyn Maud Keppel, daughter of Colonel Edward George Keppel,[11] and secondly Violet Margaret Dawson-Greene, daughter of Colonel Henry Dawson Greene.

Thomas Edward Anson, the 4th Earl of Lichfield died in 1960. He was succeeded as the 5th Earl by his grandson, (Thomas) Patrick John Anson, who was better known as Patrick Lichfield, the photographer.[12] The unfortunate timing referred to in the title of this chapter was the death of the 5th Earl's father in 1958, two years before his own father. As part of a legitimate tax planning exercise, the 4th Earl had passed assets to his son. However, because the 4th Earl's son died first before he could pass these assets on to his own son, the 5th Earl, there was a substantial tax bill to pay on the estate of the 4th Earl's son. Then two years' later, the 4th Earl died, the consequence being a second substantial tax bill. This disastrous financial calamity led to the transfer of the Shugborough estate to the National Trust in lieu of tax. Shugborough is now administered by Staffordshire County Council on behalf of the National Trust.

During the 20th century, there was a literary connection with Shugborough - J R R Tolkien, the author of "The Lord Of The Rings" stayed at Great Haywood for some time during World War I. [13]

Early in the 21st century, one of Thomas Anson's classical monument commissions, The Shepherd's Monument" had national media coverage due to a claim that it might hold a key to the whereabouts of the Holy Grail. Even former staff from Bletchley Park, the war-time home of those who broke the Enigma machine codes, were called upon in an attempt to solve the mysterious inscription: "D O.U.O.S.V.A.V.V. M".

Unfortunate Timing
Further Notes and Connections

1. William Anson, from Dunston, between Stafford and Penkridge, bought the Shugborough property from a Thomas Whitby, who had previously purchased the property from the Pagets. William Paget had acquired the Shugborough property and other extensive properties in the Trent Valley in 1546, formerly belonging to the Bishops of Lichfield, following the Dissolution of the Monasteries. The Pagets developed the bishops' former hunting lodge at Beaudesert on Cannock Chase as their family seat rather than Shugborough. For more information on the Paget family and the Dissolution of the Monasteries see, respectively, the chapter: "Here Lies The Leg" and Appendix 7: Dissolution of The Monasteries and The Reformation.

2. Despite never owning the property himself, George Anson, Admiral Lord Anson, (1697 - 1762) was a major provider of the funds, which helped to make Shugborough what it is today. His life is a story in its own right. In 1712, he enrolled in the English Navy as a volunteer. In 1717, he received his acting order as Lieutenant. Having served in the Baltic and Mediterranean, he was promoted to Captain in 1722. In 1740, with the ship "Centurion" and six other vessels, he sailed to America to fight the Spaniards and seize the "Manila Galleons" on their wealthy commercial route from Acapulco, Mexico, to the Philippines. Anson used Zihuatanejo Bay as a hiding and resting place for his crew. In 1744, after more than three years at sea and a circumnavigation of the globe, he arrived back to England with just one ship and only 145 men out of the original 1,000 that set out with him but with treasures worth more than £800,000 sterling pounds of that time – equivalent to over £100 million by 2003. No navy commander ever exceeded this fortune in loot. The success of Anson's mission resulted in his promotion to Rear Admiral. In 1747, the British fleet under Admiral Anson defeated the French, led by Admiral La Jonquiere, at the Battle of Cape Finnisterre. A series of running fights ended with all French warships sunk or captured, the most important prize being the surrender of L'Invincible, which became "The Invincible" in the service of the Royal Navy. She was the first of a completely new class of battle ship,

which was to dominate the oceans, in the service of all major navies of the world, for over 100 years. It has been said that Lord Anson, who became an Admiral of the Fleet in 1761, one year before his death, was the pre-eminent sailor of his generation - as effective at administration as he was commanding at sea.

3. Anson County, once the largest in the U.S. state of North Carolina, with a border on the Mississippi River, was carved from Bladen County in 1750. It was named after Admiral Lord Anson.

4. Eight monuments of national importance are situated in the 900 acres of Shugborough parkland. Built by Thomas Wright of Durham and James "Athenian" Stuart during the mid 18th Century, these monuments reflect the English landowner's fascination with classical architecture of the time. Thomas Anson was a founder member of the Society of Dilettanti, which was founded in 1732 and sponsored the study of fine arts such as Greek classical art. Probably the most famous founder member of this society was Sir Francis Dashwood, who was also the founder of the Hell-fire Club.

5. When Thomas Anson inherited the Shugborough estate in 1720, the Ansons were locally important but did not compare in status with their neighbours: the Pagets of Beaudesert, the Astons of Tixall and the Chetwynds of Ingestre - for more information on these families see, respectively, the chapters: "Here Lies The Leg", "What's In A Family Name?" and "The Premier Earls". Also living adjacent to Shugborough were another large land-owning family, the Wolseleys of Wolseley - see the chapter: "This Land Was My Land". Viscount Anson was the son-in-law of Thomas William Coke, the noted agriculturist universally known as Coke of Norfolk, who was created the 1st Earl of Leicester of the 7th creation.

6. In addition to Viscount Anson's Park Farm at Shugborough, the model farm of 1,600 acres of Earl Talbot (Chetwynd family) at Ingestre, the Earl of Harrowby's at Sandon with buildings designed by Samuel Wyatt, the Earl of Bradford's at Weston with its great Palladian barn, Sir John Wrottesley's at Wrottesley and Sir George Pigot's of 1,200 acres at Patshull were among the best-run agricultural enterprises in England.

7. Apart from his general extravagance, the cause of the 1st Earl of Lichfield's financial difficulties seem to have been the cost of political expenses, buying land and horse-racing. In the 18th century, substantial landowners felt it necessary to build up their political influence in the

areas where they had their country houses.

8. Augustus Henry Archibald Anson, the third son of the 1st Earl of Lichfield, was awarded a posthumous Victoria Cross for his actions in South India during the Indian Mutiny.

9. It has been claimed that Lady Louisa Mary Anne Anson, the eldest daughter of the 1st Earl, provided the inspiration for the nickname for the lavatory when her namecard was taken from her bedroom door and put it on the guest lavatory. Unfortunately, although a good story, there are many equally plausible competing claims to the origin of the word 'loo'. One of the alternative possible origins refers to the trade name 'Waterloo', which appeared prominently displayed on the iron cisterns in many British outhouses during the early 20th century.

10. For a further discussion on the impact of the agricultural depression of the 1870s and other factors, which had an adverse effect on the English Country House see Appendix 3: The Demise Of The English Country House.

11. Evelyn Maud Keppel, the first wife of the 4th Earl of Lichfield and the grandmother of Patrick Lichfield, the photographer and 5th Earl, was a direct descendant of Arnold Joost van Keppel, 1st Earl of Albermarle, a close companion of William III of England. She shares this distinction with the Duchess of Cornwall (formerly Camilla Parker Bowles). In turn, the Duchess of Cornwall is a direct descendant of Charles Lennox, 1st Duke of Lennox, the illegitimate son of Charles II, by his mistress Louise-Renée de Penancoët de Kérouaille, Duchess of Portsmouth. She shares this ancestry with the late Diana, Princess of Wales.

12. Patrick Lichfield, 5th Earl of Lichfield, the well-known photographer, died on 11 November 2005 and was interred in the family vault in the church of St Michael and All Angels, Colwich, which is near to the Shugborough estate. The family vault is hidden away behind the choir pews. This church is rich in various references to members of the aristocracy with local connections, including members of the Wolseley family (see the chapter: "This Land Was My Land"), the Chetwynds (see the chapter: "The Premier Earls") as well as the Ansons, Lord Lichfield's family.

13. The newly married JRR Tolkien and his wife took a cottage in Great Haywood where he convalesced after action in the Somme in France during the First World War. Throughout this time he was actively writing his tales and creating his magical kingdoms. One such tale,

"The Tale of the Sun and the Moon" in "The Book of Lost Tales" makes reference to the village of Tavrobel. JRR's son, Christopher Tolkien, says that the village was based on Great Haywood. Tavrobel stands by a bridge where the rivers meet and is a clear reference to the Essex Bridge at the confluence of the rivers Sow and Trent. In the tale, Eriol is encouraged to "sojourn a while in Tavrobel" and it is suggested to him that he takes up the hospitality of a gnome called Gilfanon "whose ancient house - the house of a hundred chimneys, stands nigh the bridge of Tavrobel". It is probable that Shugborough Hall is the model for this ancient house as it boasts a considerable number of chimneys and, with all the fires lit, it could have evoked a magical sight across the park when viewed from the public footpath on a misty winter's day during his convalescence.

Unfortunate Timing
Acknowledgements

Robinson, John Martin (1989), *Shugborough,* The National Trust; ISBN 070780101X

Staffordshire County Council website:

http://www.staffordshire.gov.uk/portal/page?_pageid=47,1&_dad=portal&_schema=PORTAL (accessed 2005)

This Land Was My Land

Sir Charles Wolseley, the 11th baronet, inherited the Wolseley estate on the death of his grandfather, Sir Edric, in 1953. Sir Charles was 10 at the time. Although the estate was still substantial, it was a shadow of the estate the Wolseleys held at the time of Henry VIII's Reformation.

In 1965, the old Wolseley Hall, which had fallen into a state beyond repair, was demolished, a fate suffered by many country houses in the 20th century. [1]

Nothing much happened for the next twenty years. Then, May 1990 saw the opening of Britain's first permanent garden on a grand scale to be created specifically for the public in the 20th century. It was the vision of Sir Charles and Lady Wolseley, whose aim was to create a series of gardens in a mature and tranquil setting.

Four years in the making, Wolseley Garden Park was designed to become one of the great gardens of the world and a major tourist attraction.

Unfortunately, the dream was never fulfilled but turned into a nightmare for the Wolseleys. Over £1 million was spent getting the garden ready but recession was looming. Then a tourist board grant failed to materialise. A further £150,000 went towards building the roundabout, which gives access to the Garden Park and the garden centre now owned by Wyevale. In early 1992, it was revealed that Sir Charles' business debts had risen to £4.6 million. Administrators were then appointed to supervise the running of the business.

In February 1996, the estate was put up for sale. Particulars of the sale, demanded by the National Westminster Bank and other creditors, gave the entire estate a guide price of £6.25 million.

It is said that there have been Wolseleys at Wolseley since before the Norman Conquest in 1066 and that the name is derived from the Anglo Saxon words 'wolves' and 'ley' meaning water meadow and was taken from the location rather than given to it. If these facts are correct, the Wolseley family is the oldest Staffordshire family in this book. The first family member mentioned in writing is said to be Siward, Lord of Wisele (Debretts), from whom was descended Edric, who was living in 1087.

Legend has it that early Wolseleys cleared the area of wolves, which infested the forest of Cannock Chase and preyed upon sheep and cattle grazing in the leys of the Trent Valley.

In 1297, Sir Richard Wolseley married the daughter of Roger Aston of Great Haywood Hall. [2] Her father gave her all of his lands at Bishton next to what is now called Wolseley Bridge, near Colwich, the first of a string of three villages, followed by Little Haywood and, finally, Great Haywood.

The family crest consists of a wolf's head out of a coronet. The wolves disappeared centuries ago but deer still roam freely over large areas of the area. In 1469, Edward IV granted Ralph de Wolseley the right to empark deer and a licence to construct deer leaps [3], a right the family still maintains. In the same year, Ralph was granted the right to fortify Wolseley Hall.

The Wolseleys also had the privilege granted by the Crown of owning swans, the Wolseley mark being two notches on the left side of the beak.[4]

The Wolseley Estate was at its most extensive at the time of the Reformation in Henry VIII's reign, covering in excess of 10,000 acres. However, the main branch of the Wolseley family remained staunchly Catholic. Consequently, the heavy fines imposed upon them cost them large parts of the estate. In 1629, the remaining estate passed to a prosperous Protestant cousin, Robert Wolseley, who had become the first baronet on 24 November 1628. However, the Civil War caused the family fortunes to suffer again when the estate was sequestered by Parliament because of Sir Robert's support for King Charles I. Sir Robert, who died on 21 September 1646, is commemorated by an altar tomb close by the church tower in St Michael's & All Angels Church at Colwich.

The second baronet, Sir Charles, was a Parliamentarian, who was appointed a Protectorial Councillor during the Commonwealth period. He became an intimate friend and close advisor of Oliver Cromwell, who often stayed at Wolseley.

The 5th baronet, Sir William, who was a grandson of the second baronet, inherited Wolseley on the death of his unmarried uncle, Sir Henry. Sir William was a Gentleman of the Privy Chamber to both George II and George III, which meant that he frequently spent time at one or the other of his two London houses. Following the death of his first wife, Anne, from smallpox, Sir William secretly married Anna Whitby in September 1752. Anna was a widow, who had inherited a considerable fortune on the death of her husband, also from smallpox. Whether Anna was a willing party to the marriage and whether Sir William married for love or money will never be known for certain. However, one fact about this affair is unequivocal - it resulted in one of the most sensational trials of the 18th century. Besides Sir William, Anna had another suitor, Stafford barrister, John Robins, who had been M.P. for Stafford. After her marriage to Sir William, Anna 'married' John Robins at Castlechurch, Stafford, persuading the vicar to enter 16 June 1752 as the marriage date in the parish register, thereby pre-dating her marriage to Sir William. On 12 October, Sir William was informed that his new bride was already married and wished to have no further contact with him. Worse was to come a few days later when papers were delivered from the High Court in London informing Sir William that he was being charged with having drugged Anna and marrying her in the middle of the night against her wishes. In addition, John Robins went to court declaring that he was Anne's legal husband and Sir William filed for divorce. The ecclesiastic courts also became involved in the case. John Robins eventually faced charges of perjury, fled abroad and died in debt in 1754.

In 1792, the 7th baronet, another Charles, married his first wife, Mary Clifford of Tixall. [2] Shortly afterwards, they went to live in France, Charles having become a confirmed Francophile during his Grand Tour [5] of the Continent. After Mary died in 1811, Sir Charles married Anne Wright from Essex. When his father died in 1817, Sir Charles returned to England and became actively involved in the movement for Parliamentary Reform. This was a period of unrest throughout the country and Sir Charles spoke out strongly for reform at many meetings. He was arrested after a mass meeting of at least 20,000 people held on Newhall Hill in Birmingham on 12 July 1819. At this meeting, he had been selected as a 'legislatorial attorney'[6,7] and directed to attempt to take a seat in the House of Commons as Member for Birmingham with a mandate to require annual parliaments and the ballot. At that time, many populous areas were unrepresented in Parliament. Eventually, Sir Charles was jailed for 18 months and fined £1,000. After his release from prison, Sir Charles went to live in Brussels.

Yet another Sir Charles, the 9th baronet, was a close friend of his Irish kinsman, Field Marshal Viscount Garnet Wolseley.[8,9]

The last baronet to live at Wolseley Hall was Sir Edric, the 10th baronet. He raised six children there during the war torn years. His eldest son and heir, Stephen, was killed in Normandy just after D-Day. [10] Stephen's infant son, Charles, became heir to Wolseley and, as noted earlier, succeeded his grandfather, Edric, in 1953.

This Land Was My Land
Further Notes and Connections

1. For more information on the loss of country houses in England, see Appendix 3: The Demise of the English Country House.

2. The Wolseley and Aston/Clifford families have been joined in marriage on several occasions. See also the chapter: "What's In A Family Name?"

3. Deer leaps allowed deer to enter a deer park but prevented them from getting out, thus ensuring the introduction of new blood to the herds within. Following introduction by the monarchy, the passion for parks soon spread to the great figures of state and then to the lesser nobility. It was necessary to obtain a licence to create a new park but during the period of strong economic growth through the 13th century there was no shortage of applicants. There was certainly an element of demonstrating one's status and wealth but the main pressure behind the development of deer parks was economic. Although some landowners maintained their parks as examples of 'conspicuous consumption' and did not expect a huge return from what was often marginal land other, perhaps better-managed, estates ran their deer on an industrial scale.

4. At Longdon, between Rugeley and Lichfield, there is a public house called 'The Swan With Two Necks' - this is a corruption of 'the swan with two nicks', which is also the mark of the Worshipful Company of Vintners, a once powerful guild which owned land and houses all over England. The Crown granted privileges of keeping swans on open and common waters provided they were marked. All unmarked swans belong to the Crown.

5. The English upper classes regarded the Grand Tour as such an indispensable part of a young man's education that a prolonged tour was often substituted for a college education rather than being a mere addendum to a college degree. Consequently, a tutor often accompanied the young traveller and supervised his lessons and conduct. The Grand Tour particularly emphasised France and Italy, which were much admired, but also nearly always included highly civilized Vienna.

6. The meeting in Birmingham, at which Sir Charles Wolseley (7th Baronet) was selected as a legislatorial attorney, preceded the more

famous meeting on 16 August 1819 at St Peter's Field, Manchester, the outcome of which has become known as the Peterloo Massacre. This event generated much anger towards the government particularly from radical groups such as the Spenceans. Arthur Thistlewood, one of this group, was reported to have said, "High Treason was committed against the people at Manchester. I resolved that the lives of the instigators of massacre should atone for the souls of murdered innocents." The consequence was The Cato Street Conspiracy, the objective of which was to assassinate members of the British Government, whilst they were dining at the Earl of Harrowby's London home, 39 Grosvenor Square in February 1820. For more information on the Earls of Harrowby, see the chapter: "A Near Escape For A Road Builder".

7. The year 1819 was a turning point in the relationship between the state and liberty of opinion. The extraordinary growth of manufacturing resulting from the Industrial Revolution had suddenly brought together vast populations without affection and traditional respect for their employers. Revolutionaries and radical elements of a developing press easily influenced such people.

8. Field Marshal Viscount Garnet Wolseley (1833 - 1913) was one of the greatest generals of the 19th century. A highly efficient commander with an admiring public, Wolseley was employed by successive governments as chief troubleshooter of the British Empire. Back in Egypt in 1884, he organised and headed an expedition to the Nile to rescue his friend General Charles 'Chinese' Gordon, besieged at Khartoum in the Sudan. An advance party arrived on 28 January 1885, two days after the city had fallen and Gordon had been killed. For his efforts, Wolseley was elevated to viscount, which, by special remainder, devolved on his only daughter upon his death. An indication of his popularity was that Gilbert & Sullivan's 'model of a modern Major-General' in the 'Pirates of Penzance' was always dressed up to look like him. He wrote the forerunner of modern army training manuals. As well as being a brilliant general, he was a military reformer, whose work formed the basis of the modern British Army. After his death, his widow had a memorial to the Field Marshal placed in St Michael's & All Angels Church, Colwich, in recognition of his close ties with the Wolseley ancestral home. Garnet Wolseley was descended from the 2nd baronet's youngest son, Richard Wolseley. Richard served William III in Ireland and purchased an estate, which became known as Mount Wolseley - the house has now become the club house of an international

standard golf course. Richard's third son, another Richard, was created a baronet in 1745 during the reign of George II, thus establishing the Irish cadet baronetage branch of the Wolseley family.

9.   Viscount Wolseley's youngest brother, Frederick York Wolseley, went to Australia where he invented electric fencing and the mechanical sheepshearer, founding the Wolseley Sheep Shearing Machine Company Ltd in Sydney in 1887. He returned to Britain in 1889, eventually setting up the Wolseley Tool & Motor Car Company Ltd in Birmingham. One of his early employees was Herbert Austin, who resigned in 1905 to start the Austin Motor Company Ltd in Longbridge.

10.   In 1955, the widow of Captain Stephen Garnet Hubert Francis Wolseley, RA, who had died of wounds received in action in 1944, was granted the style, title, place and precedence, as if her late husband had survived and succeeded to the title of baronet i.e. Pamela, Lady Wolseley. In 1953, their son, Charles had succeeded as 11th baronet on the death of his grandfather, Sir Edric. For more information on etiquette, correct form et.c. see Appendix 1: Hereditary Titles.

This Land Was My Land
Acknowledgements

Wolseley, Imogene (2003), *Wolseley - a thousand years of history*, The Lichfield Press; ISBN 0905985346

Staffordshire Advertiser

Staffordshire Newsletter

Daily Mail

Daily Telegraph

The Cromwell Association and the Cromwell Museum, Huntingdon

What's In A Family Name?

Most of us are used to taking our father's name on birth and, only in the case of daughters do we normally expect this to change on marriage to that of the husband. But this is not always so, especially if substantial inheritances are at stake, as the following tale will show. Be prepared to be confused on first reading but persevere, as the story is fascinating.

This story starts with Edward Aston (1494-1568) a prominent Staffordshire Protestant, who built an Elizabethan hall [1] at Tixall, near Stafford, in 1555. He had married well: first to Mary Vernon, daughter of Sir Henry Vernon, who died without issue in 1525, and then to Jane or Joan, daughter of Sir Thomas Bowles/Bolles of Penhow in Monmouthshire.

His son, Sir Walter Aston [2] (1529-89), another prominent Staffordshire Protestant, built Tixall Gatehouse around 1580. In August 1586, the Hall was the temporary prison of Mary, Queen of Scots, while her quarters at Chartley [3] were being searched for incriminating evidence.

Sir Walter's grandson, Walter was created the 1st Lord Aston of Forfar on 28 November 1627.[4] He was sent to Spain as Ambassador from 1620 - 1625 to try and arrange a marriage between the Infanta daughter of Philip III, and Charles, Prince of Wales. During his second visit from 1635-38, he became a Roman Catholic. Catholic landowners like the rest of the 'gentry' wished to make 'suitable' matches for their sons and daughters. Unfortunately for the Catholics, their numbers were decreasing while they remained subject to draconian laws about inheriting property and paying fines for non-attendance at Church of England services among other difficulties.[5] Consequently, Catholic families are very inter-connected, as we will see later.

In 1729, Walter, 4th Lord Aston, began to take down and rebuild Tixall Hall. After his death in 1744, his son, James, 5th Lord Aston, continued this work. Unfortunately, James died young in 1751, aged 28, leaving two young daughters, and an unfinished Hall.

Barbara, the younger daughter, [6] married the Hon. Thomas Clifford, 4th son of Hugh, 3rd Lord Clifford of Chudleigh, in 1761.[7] She inherited Tixall when she came of age in 1768, and Thomas set about building a new house and improving the estate as well as bringing up a family.[8,9]

The new house incorporated the rebuilt east wing and quadrangle, with an impressive new range at the front as shown in an undated ground plan found at Burton Constable Hall in East Yorkshire.

In 1821, Thomas Clifford's son, Thomas Hugh, inherited the Burton Constable Estates, in the East Riding of Yorkshire, near Hull through a somewhat circuitous route. On inheritance, he assumed by sign-manual, the surname and arms of Constable only.

In order to trace this route, we need to go back to 1620 when Sir Henry Constable, a knight, of Burton Constable, was created Viscount Dunbar. The order of succession following him is not clear. Some documents indicate that John, Robert, and William, sons of the second viscount successively held the title. According to Dr David Connell, Director of the Burton Constable Foundation, there were four or five Viscounts Dunbar, depending on how it is interpreted. The problem arose in the mid-seventeenth century when Robert Constable, 2nd Viscount Dunbar, died in 1666. John, the new (3rd) Viscount was a minor and died shortly after inheriting, to be succeeded by his brother, another Robert. Dr Connell is not sure what the precise rules were, but 19th century pedigrees suggested only four Viscounts, with Robert being regarded as the third Viscount Dunbar. Perhaps there is some other reason for this incertitude yet to be discovered or revealed?

When William, the last (4th or 5th?) Viscount Dunbar, [10] died in 1718 without legal issue, he left the estates to Cuthbert Tunstall, his sister's son, upon condition that Cuthbert should take the name of Constable. Cuthbert was the son of Francis Tunstall of Wycliffe Hall, Yorkshire, England, and Cicely, daughter of John Constable, second Viscount Dunbar. Cuthbert Constable was twice married, first to Amy, fifth daughter of Hugh, 3rd Lord Clifford, by whom he had four children, William (1), who died young, William (2), Cicely, and Winefred, and secondly to Elizabeth Heneage, by whom he had one son, Marmaduke, who inherited the estate of Wycliffe and resumed the family name of Tunstall.

William Constable, the next owner, who died without issue in 1791, entailed the estates on Edward and Francis Sheldon, sons of his sister, Cecily, and after them on Thomas Hugh Clifford. Thomas Hugh was created a baronet in 1814, and, in 1821, succeeded to the Constable estates when Francis Sheldon died without surviving issue, his only child, Maria, having died in 1810.

When Thomas Hugh's son, Thomas Aston Clifford Constable (known as Clifford) succeeded in 1823 he was still a minor, and for a time preferred his own ancestral home at Tixall. However, following his marriage to his cousin, Marianne (Mary Anne) Chichester, in 1827 and an extended honeymoon travelling in Europe, he decided to consolidate his estates in Yorkshire and put Tixall up for sale in 1833. It failed to meet the reserve and was eventually sold in 1845 to Earl Talbot of neighbouring Ingestre.[11] Tixall Hall was then rented out. The hall was eventually taken down around 1926. [12]

Thomas Aston Clifford Constable's son was also called Thomas. His son, the last baronet, was called Frederick Augustus Talbot Clifford Constable (known as Talbot).

For the next twist in the tale, we need to go back to Mary Barbara Constable, the daughter of Thomas Hugh Clifford Constable. In 1826, she married a cousin, Sir Charles Chichester.[13] Their eldest son, Charles Raleigh Chichester (d.1891), was educated at Stonyhurst College.[14] In 1852, he married Mary Josephine Balfe (d.1871), co-heir to the estates of James Balfe in County Roscommen. Their eldest son, Lt. Col Walter George Raleigh Chichester, succeeded to the Irish estates in 1891, and then, in 1894, to that of Burton Constable, upon the death of Sir Frederick Augustus Talbot Clifford Constable.

In 1895, Walter George assumed the name of Constable by royal licence and became known as Chichester-Constable.

To add to all this confusion, we already know that Mary Barbara Constable's brother, Sir Thomas Aston Clifford Constable, had married Sir Charles Chichester's sister, Marianne Chichester - so brother and sister had married sister and brother, who were also cousins!

Burton Constable remained in the possession of the Chichester-Constable family until 1992 when the house and parklands were handed over to the Burton Constable Foundation. This secured the long-term future of the house and its collections. The family continue to occupy one wing of the house but with yet another twist along the female line.

What's In A Family Name?
Further Notes and Connections

1. The Elizabethan hall built at Tixall in 1555 by Edward Aston and the later hall, on which work began in 1729, both use stone quarried from the estate quarries as did the Tixall Gatehouse, which still stands today and is now used as a holiday let by the Landmark Trust. Tixall Stone was renowned for resisting the action of water and the building of Staffordshire and Worcestershire Canal, which ran about 1/2 mile east of the quarry and was completed in 1772, firstly provided a new use for the stone in the construction of locks and other canal buildings and then provided easy transport for the stone. For example, in 1781, Tixall Stone was used for the battlements and balustrades of John Gwyn's new bridge over the Severn at Worcester. Earl Talbot of the neighbouring Ingestre estate purchased the Tixall estate in 1845 - see also the chapter: "The Premier Earls".

2. Jane, the daughter of Sir Walter Aston (1529-89), married William Crompton of Stone Park, Stone, Staffordshire. Their tomb was originally on the south side of the chancel of the parish church of Stone, which had been rebuilt in 1572. Unfortunately, It is now to be found in a dilapidated and eroded state in the churchyard of the present parish church of St Michael and St Wulfad, Stone, which was built between 1753 and 1758. William Crompton's father, another William, had acquired lands formerly belonging to Stone Priory following its dissolution. Along with Trentham and Ranton, Stone Priory was among the first Staffordshire monastic houses to be dissolved. See also Appendix 7: Dissolution of the Monasteries and The Reformation for a brief discourse on these related events and their impact on the country's development.

3. Chartley is a few miles away from Tixall on the road to Uttoxeter, pronounced by old Staffordshire folk as 'Utcheter'. Mary, Queen of Scots, had been moved to Chartley in 1585. Sir Francis Walsingham, Queen Elizabeth's spymaster, knew she had been plotting again, this time with increasing desperation. The failure of the Throckmorton Plot had shaken her badly, though she professed innocence of any involvement. Her exact role in that conspiracy remains unclear; it is

possible she only knew of it, but did not actively encourage it. However, she did enthusiastically support the treason of another English Catholic, a young man named Sir Anthony Babington. Babington was only a half-hearted conspirator, but Walsingham was content to use him to lure Mary into a final trap. He sensed this was his best opportunity to secure enough evidence to finally convince Elizabeth of her cousin's complicity. The queen's refusal to condemn Mary was no longer a benevolent quirk; for her councillors, it was a matter of life and death. Walsingham had soon collected a number of letters between Mary, Babington and others. In one of these, Mary explicitly approved the murder of Elizabeth. This was the letter that Walsingham needed. When confronted with it, Elizabeth was at first disbelieving and then angry. Mary was arrested and eventually taken to Fotheringhay Castle where she was tried and later executed in February 1587. Some accounts say that, after her arrest, Mary was taken to Tixall before being taken back to Chartley Hall from which she was moved to Fotheringhay. See also the chapter: "The Premier Earls", as the 6th Earl of Shrewsbury had had the unenviable job of being the warder of Mary, Queen of Scots, for many years.

4. Walter, 1st Lord Aston of Forfar, died on 13 August 1639 at age 55. He was buried at St. Mary's, Stafford.

5. Those refusing to participate in Church of England services were known as 'recusants'. The term did not only apply to Roman Catholics. See also Appendix 8: Glossary of Terms.

6. Mary, the elder daughter of the 5th Lord Aston, was married at Worksop, Nottinghamshire, in 1766 to her cousin, Walter Blount, of Mawley Hall, Shropshire, and Sodington, Worcestershire, sometimes spelt Soddington in old documents. She inherited the Aston estate at Colton, Staffordshire - see the chapter: "Colton's Lost Country House". Although in different counties, Mawley, near Cleobury Mortimer, and Sodington are within five miles of one another.

7. Members of the Clifford family have been very prominent in English history - further information on Thomas Clifford, 4th son of the 3rd Lord Clifford of Chudleigh, and other more notable Cliffords is given in Appendix 4: The Cliffords.

8. On 13 December 1792, Thomas and Barbara Clifford's daughter, Mary, married Charles Wolseley of Wolseley Hall near Colwich - see also the chapter: "This Land Was My Land". The marriage took place at the Anglican church at Tixall as the 1753 Marriage Act had decreed

that no one could be legally married except by a Church of England minister. Mary and Edward Blount, aunt and cousin of the bride, were two of the witnesses - yet more of the ubiquitous Blounts - see also Appendix 5: The Blounts.

9.   During the period 1810 - 1818, it is documented that the Rt Hon Viscount Granville, MP for Stafford, rented Tixall Hall, during which time two of his children were baptised at the parish church. Viscount Granville was a member of the Leveson-Gower family - see also the chapter: "The Earl Who Washed His Own Socks". During this period, Thomas and Mary Clifford were residing in Bath as Mary suffered from rheumatism.

10. The wife of William, the 4th or 5th Viscount Dunbar, was Elizabeth Clifford, the eldest daughter of Hugh, 2nd Lord Clifford of Chudleigh - see also Note 6 above and Appendix 4: The Cliffords. After William's death in 1718, she married again in 1720, the bridegroom being Charles Gregory, 9th and last Viscount Fairfax of Emley of Gilling Castle, Yorkshire. However, she died of smallpox in April 1721 and is buried at Bath Abbey.

11. In 1856, the 3rd Earl Talbot, an Admiral and Lord in Waiting to Queen Victoria, succeeded his distant cousin as the 18th Earl of Shrewsbury & Waterford - Premier Earl of England and Ireland. See also the chapter: "The Premier Earls".

12. It has been recorded that some of the stone was used at St John's Roman Catholic Church at Great Haywood. However, another report states that it was used to build the chancel at St John's Anglican Church at Littleworth, Stafford. In fact, there is some truth in both reports. When the estate was sold in 1845, the Cliffords gave an acre of land at Great Haywood, along with the Catholic Chapel completed in 1828, to the local Catholics, who arranged for it to be moved from Tixall to Great Haywood - see also Note 13. In the following century, the then Earl of Shrewsbury donated land at Littleworth along with stone from Tixall Hall, which was demolished around 1926. St John's Church and School were built on this site, the Tixall Hall stone being used to build the vestry and chancel of the church. The two coad stone lions from the top of the single storey wings, were sold to the Lilleshall Estate for £5 and once guarded the entrance to the National Sports Centre at Lilleshall. Their current whereabouts has not been ascertained but two old and rather worn stone lions are to be found on the old Wellington road, close to Lilleshall village. Richard Davies, a long-time inhabitant

of the cottage close to the present location of these lions, remembers them being in their present location from around 1966. He was also told that they were two of four lions, which were at the base of the Lilleshall monument, erected in memory of the 1st Duke of Sutherland. Could these be the lions or could they be the other two lions, which were at the base of the monument? Perhaps, none of these four lions are the Tixall lions?

13. Mary Barbara Constable and Sir Charles Chichester were married on 13 April 1826 at Tixall Church, near Stafford. As noted in the main text, the following year, Mary's brother, Thomas Aston Clifford Constable, married Charles' sister, Marianne (Mary Anne) again at Tixall Church. This latter wedding, held on 27 September 1827, was, in fact, a double wedding, the other couple being Isabella Constable, sister of Thomas and Mary Barbara, and Henry Arundell. It is most likely that this official ceremony complemented a large Catholic Nuptial Mass, possibly held in the original private chapel at Tixall Hall. In the same year, Sir Thomas commissioned Joseph Ireland to build a new chapel, adjoining the south wing of Tixall Hall and behind the Tixall Gatehouse. This was the first time that Roman Catholics were allowed to have a freestanding chapel. Building work was completed in 1828.

14. Stonyhurst, which is set in a rural Lancashire estate, was given to the Roman Catholic order of the Jesuits by Thomas Weld, a former pupil of St Omer in northern France. St Omer was founded in 1593 to provide a Catholic education for English families unable to educate their children in the Roman Catholic faith at home. The college moved to Bruges in 1762, then Liège in 1773 before its final move to Stonyhurst in 1794.

What's In A Family Name?
Acknowledgements

Andrews, Anne (1995), *A History of Tixall - 1. Tixall's Churches,* Hanyards Press; ISBN 0952742519

Clifford, Hugh (1987), *The House of Clifford,* Phillimore & Co; ISBN 0850336341

Cope, Norman A (1972), *Stone in Staffordshire - The History of a Market Town,* Wood, Mitchell & Co

Andrews, Anne http://pages.britishlibrary.net/tixandrews/tixall/txgths.html (accessed 2004)

Connell, Dr David, and the Burton Constable Foundation

Titles Move In Mysterious Ways

Few English titles and family descents are as complicated as those of the Barony of Stafford. Since the time of the Norman Conquest in 1066, the Stafford descent has meandered via female heiresses through five families: the Norman de Toenis, the Bagots, a cadet line of the Howards, the Jerninghams and the Fitzherberts. However, one common thread has run from the de Toenis all the way to the Fitzherberts - the ownership of Stafford Castle.

From early in the 13th century, the Staffords embarked on a journey, which saw them rise to great magnate status becoming premier dukes as well as large landowners in 24 counties of England as well as the Marches of Wales. This expansion from their original base in Staffordshire was the result of a number of marriages to great heiresses and of successful careers in the Hundred Years' War against France, which provided ample opportunities for enrichment and advancement.

This rise could be said to have started with Robert de Stafford, who, in about 1240, married Alice Corbet, through whom eventually came the Lordship of Caus on the Shropshire/Montgomery border but this would not be until around 1346.

Robert's son, Edmund, 1st Lord Stafford, (1273-1308), made the first of the family's marriages to even more substantial heiresses. His wife, Margaret, who was the daughter of Ralph, Lord Basset, eventually inherited part of the Basset estates in Norfolk and the Midlands. Edmund's son, Ralph (1301-1372) built on his inheritance through his military service to Edward III (r 1327-1377), especially in the Hundred Years' War, and his two marriages, in particular, his second marriage to Margaret Audley, one of the heiresses to the estate of her grandfather, Gilbert de Clare, Earl of Gloucester and Hereford, one of the most powerful nobles of early mediaeval England.[1] The de Clares had profited from playing a major role in Edward I's conquest of Wales in the 1270s and 1280s; much of the land taken from the Welsh Princes was bestowed upon the de Clares. In addition, Margaret's father, Hugh Audley, settled all his Audley properties on Ralph, Margaret and their heirs. In 1346, Ralph came into this huge inheritance along with the Lordship of Caus. Margaret's inheritance included large estates in Tonbridge, Kent, and Thornbury, Gloucestershire.[2] In 1348,

Ralph gained further distinction when he became one of the Founder Knights of the Garter.[3] As further evidence of his heightened status and new wealth, Ralph was created Earl of Stafford by Edward III on 5 March 1350/1. Ralph died on 31 August 1372 at Tonbridge Castle, part of his Audley inheritance and was buried at the local priory of Tonburton. During his lifetime, he had founded the Austin Friars in Stafford in 1344 and continued the family benefaction of Stone Priory, where many of the early Staffords were buried since its founding by Robert de Stafford after the Norman Conquest.

Hugh, his second son, became the 2nd Earl of Stafford in 1372.[4] Like his father, he gained distinction in the French Wars and, in 1375, was also made a Knight of the Garter. Hugh served Richard II (r 1377-1399) as a councillor. His eldest son, Ralph, was murdered in 1385 by Richard II's half-brother, John Holland, Earl of Huntingdon, later Duke of Exeter, who was also a great grandson of Edward I. Embittered by Richard reneging on his promise not to pardon Holland, Hugh decided to leave England on a pilgrimage to Jerusalem. After his death in Rhodes in 1386 whilst returning from the Holy Land, his body was brought home and buried at Stone Priory.

Hugh's youngest son, Edmund, the 5th Earl of Stafford, made the greatest of the family's marriages when, in 1398, he married Anne Plantagenet, the daughter of Thomas of Woodstock.[5] Anne had briefly been married (at the age of 9) to Edmund's elder brother, Thomas, the 3rd Earl of Stafford, who died young like his brother, William, the 4th Earl. Anne, the daughter of Eleanor de Bohun, was heiress to the Earldom of Buckingham [6], half of the de Bohun estates [7] and the office of Lord High Constable of England, one of the Great Offices of State.[8] Anne's inheritance was larger than anything the Staffords had so far acquired by inheritance, warfare and marriage. Edmund died in 1403 and Anne died in 1438 after which their son, Humphrey, was known as Earl of Buckingham.

On 14 September 1444, Humphrey was created 1st Duke of Buckingham. This was made possible through his royal descent [9] as great-grandson and heir-general of Edward III as well as a lifetime's service to the Crown and being one of the richest and most powerful landowners in England.[10] In 1447, he capped his creation as a duke by securing a special grant of precedence before all dukes of subsequent creation except those of the royal blood. His wife, Anne Neville [11], daughter of Ralph Neville, 1st Earl of Westmoreland, was also of royal descent from Edward III through her mother, Joan (de) Beaufort, daughter of John of Gaunt, Duke of Lancaster, a son of Edward III.

Almost immediately following his ducal creation, he was caught up in the troubles, which eventually led to what became known as the Wars of the Roses (1455-85). At the Battle of St Albans in 1455, Humphrey, who had remained loyal to the Lancastrian Henry VI, was wounded but his eldest son, Humphrey, Earl of Stafford, was killed. Humphrey, the 1st Duke, lasted another five years before being killed at the Battle of Northampton - a brilliant career, capped by a dukedom, had ended in failure.

The 1st Duke's son, Humphrey, Earl of Stafford, had married Margaret Beaufort, daughter and heiress of the Lancastrian, Edmund, Duke of Somerset, who was also killed at the Battle of St Albans. The Duke of Somerset, who was a great-grandson of Edward III, was married to Eleanor Beauchamp, daughter of Richard, Earl of Warwick, the most powerful supporter of the Yorkist, Edward IV. Consequently, Humphrey's son, Henry, who became the 2nd Duke of Buckingham at the age of 5 on his grandfather's death, straddled the Lancastrian/Yorkist dynastic divide.

However, these marriages, which gave the 2nd Duke of Buckingham a triple descent from Edward III, were partly instrumental in the undoing of the Staffords - such families of royal descent were seen as possible threats to the Crown during such a period of instability. During the period from 1460, when the 2nd Duke inherited his title, until he died in 1483, which cover most of the Wars of the Roses period, there were four kings with two kings reigning twice: Lancastrian Henry VI (1422-61 & 1470-71), Yorkist Edward IV (1461-70 & 1471-83), Yorkist Edward V (1483) and Yorkist Richard III (1483-85). Perhaps unwisely, but probably for reasons as basic as a need for royal favours and rewards to support his extravagant lifestyle, the 2nd Duke supported Richard, Duke of Gloucester, in his claim to the Crown. Initially, all seemed to go well: the new king, as Richard III, rewarded the 2nd Duke with grants of important offices, including the Wardenship of the Cinque Ports, which reinforced the 2nd Duke's position at the head of England's peerage. For Richard's coronation in 1483, the Duke was appointed Lord Great Chamberlain, another of the Great Offices of State. But, by the end of the year, the Duke had completed a total fall from grace, which was ended by his beheading on 2 November at Salisbury at the age of 28. This quick descent began after he had declared his support for the claim to the throne of Henry Tudor and Elizabeth of York. The Duke of Buckingham raised an army in Wales in support of Henry, who planned to invade England from France. Unfortunately, after Henry's ships ran into a storm and returned to Brittany, the Duke's army deserted him leaving him to escape to one of his Midlands estates where he was captured and taken to Salisbury. He was attainted as a traitor and his estates and titles confiscated by Richard III.

In 1485, Richard lost his crown to Henry VII at the Battle of Bosworth. The attainder against the Duke of Buckingham was immediately reversed and his eldest son, Edward, was restored to all his honours at the age of seven and became the 3rd Duke of Buckingham. At this time, he was the only extant English Duke and had by far the largest income of any English peer of his time. But this wealth, allied with his royal descent and the ambivalent behaviour of his two predecessors, made the Tudor hierarchy suspicious of him.[12]

In 1508, Henry VIII succeeded his father. As many people found to their cost, Henry had a very jealous nature. The 3rd Duke seemed to be totally oblivious of this and eventually paid the price. His downfall could be said to have begun in 1519, when he entertained Henry with dazzling splendour at Penshurst. He followed this in 1520 with an ostentatious show of wealth at the Field of the Cloth of Gold in France where Henry VIII met the French king, Francis I. He was also indiscreet, openly criticising Cardinal Wolsey, his policies and complaining about the Tudor exclusion of the nobility from political power. Furthermore, he was high-handed, arrogant and considered himself above the law. The Tudors and their ministers came to see the Duke as a disruptive force. In 1521, at the age of 43, the 3rd Duke was arrested, tried for high treason and executed on 17 May on Tower Hill. All the titles [13] were attainted by Act of Parliament in 1523 and the estates confiscated by Henry VIII.[14] The family was never to attain such pre-eminence and wealth again but drifted into obscurity, the last male Stafford dying in 1640.

In 1637, Mary Stafford,[15] the last of the Staffords, married Sir William Howard, son of the 21st Earl of Arundel.[16] Three years later, William and Mary were jointly created Baron and Baroness of Stafford (a new creation) and Viscount and Viscountess Stafford. Mary and her descendants were also heir-generals to the old Stafford peerage and any of the residual honours of the Dukes of Buckingham. As for William, he was also a descendant (great-great-great-grandson) of the 3rd Duke of Buckingham. Both Stafford and Howard families were Catholic. At the beginning of the Civil War, Viscount Stafford and his wife settled in Antwerp but he soon returned to serve Charles I.

After the civil war, his lands were sequestered because he was both Royalist and Catholic.

Just before Charles II was restored to the throne, William was chosen by the English Catholics to offer the King £100,000 if they were permitted to follow their own religion. Soon after Charles became King, William's lands were restored to him. He was often in Stafford frequently staying at Lord Aston's house at Tixall.[17]

Ever since the atrocities committed against Protestants during the reign of the Catholic 'Bloody Mary', Mary I, Catholics had been mistrusted by many English people, who feared that when Charles II died, England would become a Catholic country under James II. In 1678, Titus Oates took advantage of this paranoia to lay false charges against a number of Catholics that they were involved in plot to murder Charles II. In October of that year, Viscount Stafford was one of five peers arrested on charges of treason and imprisoned in the Tower of London to await trial by the House of Lords.

The trial lasted for five days with many witnesses and then each of the Lords present was asked for his verdict. 31 Lords voted 'Not Guilty' but 55 voted 'Guilty'. On 29 December 1680, Viscount Stafford was beheaded on Tower Hill. In May 1929, Pope Pius XI issued a decree honouring Viscount Stafford in the Roman Catholic Church as the Blessed William Howard.[18]

William Howard's son, Henry, was created Earl of Stafford and his father's lands were restored to him. In 1688, when James II fled from England to France, the Earl of Stafford went into exile with him and his family lived abroad for many years.

In 1737, George Jerningham succeeded his brother to become the 5th baronet. Sir George had been born in 1680, the same year as Viscount Stafford's execution. He spent most of his early life in continental Europe because anti-Catholic feelings were still running high. However, in 1733, he returned to Costessey, Norfolk in 1733 and married Mary Plowden, niece and heiress of the 4th and last Earl of Stafford [19] thus carrying into the Jerningham family a claim to the Barony of Stafford. He died aged 94 in 1774. His eldest son, Sir William Jerningham, succeeded him as the 6th baronet. Through his mother, he inherited the baronial castle of Stafford and considerable estates in Shropshire and Staffordshire.[20] On the death in 1807 of his cousin, Lady Anastasia Stafford-Howard, an Augustinian (Blue) nun in Paris (who would have been

Baroness Stafford in her own right but for her great-grandfather's attainder), William became heir to the remaining honours of the Stafford-Howard family but he died before establishing his claim. Sir William took an active part in the agitations, which preceded the Catholic Emancipation. He was a member of the 'Catholic Association' and was elected to represent the Midland district.

Although he was active in Catholic affairs, and in spite of the anti-Catholic feelings of the period, Sir William appeared to be popular in the 'society' of Norfolk and was a friend of the Anglican Bishop of Norwich. According to the diaries of Parson Woodforde he mixed much with the local 'Nobility and Clergy'.

His eldest son, Sir George William Jerningham, the 7th Baronet, was created 8th Baron Stafford in 1825 at which time he adopted the name Stafford-Jerningham. Lord Stafford succeeded to the ancient Barony of Stafford after the reversal of the attainder of Sir William Howard, Viscount Stafford; the House of Lords resolving on 6 July 1825: " Sir George Jerningham had made out his claim to the title, dignity and honour of Baron Stafford, under certain letters patent, bearing date 12 Sept in the 16th year of the reign of King CHARLES 1." The Baronetcy and the Barony were combined in the person of Sir George. The 9th 10th and 11th Barons all died without issue. Emily Charlotte Jerningham, sister of the 10th and 11th Barons, married Basil Thomas Fitzherbert of Swynnerton, Staffordshire, and their son, Francis Edward Fitzherbert, born in 1859, became the 12th Baron Stafford in 1913.

Besides inheriting the Barony of Stafford from his uncle, Francis Fitzherbert also inherited the landed estates in Shropshire and Staffordshire. He also inherited some of the remaining contents of Costessey Hall in Norfolk but not the hall itself nor the 3,000-acre Norfolk estate, which passed with the Jerningham baronetcy to William Jerningham, the last male member of his family, who died in 1935. By 1999, all that remained of the hall was a fragment of the ivy covered belfry tower on the Costessey Park Golf Course.

There is a table showing the line of descent of the Barony of Stafford at the end of this chapter.

Titles Move In Mysterious Ways
Further Notes and Connections

1. Although Gilbert 'The Red' de Clare died in 1295, his second marriage to Joan of Acre, the daughter of Edward 1, had given him three daughters and a son, also named Gilbert. This latter Gilbert was also a brave and fierce fighter; he loyally supported the king, and fought and died for Edward II at Bannockburn against the Scots in 1314. The three daughters were Elizabeth, the eldest, Margaret and Eleanor. Elizabeth was married three times. After the death of her last husband, she used a large portion of her remaining wealth to endow Clare College in Cambridge in 1338; if she had not done so, the College (then known as University Hall) would have closed only twelve years after its foundation. Margaret, whose second marriage was to Hugh Audley, received the Lordship of Newport and other lands across England. Margaret was first married to Piers Gaveston, close attendant of Edward II. There has been speculation that Margaret's marriage to Gaveston was intended to prevent rumour spreading as to the nature of his relationship with Edward II. Eleanor was married to Hugh le Despenser - who replaced Gaveston as Edward's favourite. Le Despenser was later beheaded with his father in 1326. Eleanor went on to marry William la Zouche.

2. Thornbury Castle, which came into the Stafford family in the 14th century, was confiscated by Henry VIII but returned by Mary I. It was eventually sold by the 2nd Earl of Stafford in 1727 to his cousin, the 8th Duke of Norfolk. By the 20th century, it had become a country house hotel.

3. It was thought that in 1344 King Edward III, inspired by the legend of King Arthur and the Knights of the Round Table, made a spectacular demonstration of his interest in Arthurian legend during a massive joust at Windsor Castle. He also promised to renew King Arthur's fraternity of knights with all the paragons of knightly virtues with a complement of 300 men. Work also even began on a gigantic circular building two hundred feet across within the upper ward of the castle to house this so-called Order of the Round Table but the renewal of war with France halted this plan. However, in 1348, Edward III revived the idea in a

different guise with the intention that this new Order of Chivalry, the Order of the Garter, would be reserved as the highest reward for loyalty and military merit. Although the original plan was to restrict the Order of the Garter to 24 knights, by 1349/50 it consisted of Edward III as Sovereign together with 25 Knights Companion, one of whom was Edward, Prince of Wales, the Black Prince. These 'founder knights', few of whom were much over the age of 30 and four were under the age of 20, were military men, skilled in battle and tournaments. The founder-knights had all served in the French campaigns of the time, including the Battle of Crécy (1346) and three were foreigners, who had previously sworn allegiance to the English king.

4. It was during the time of Hugh, 2nd Earl of Stafford (1342-86), that the Stafford family is believed to have adopted their knot symbol, which, in more recent times, has been adopted by many Staffordshire institutions, so much so that it is often erroneously referred to as the Staffordshire Knot rather than the Stafford Knot.

5. Thomas of Woodstock was the 7th and youngest son of Edward III. He was created Earl of Buckingham by his nephew, Richard II, at the latter's coronation in 1377 and, in 1385, he was created Duke of Gloucester. Thomas married Eleanor (de) Bohun, the elder daughter of Humphrey (de) Bohun, 7th Earl of Hereford, 6th Earl of Essex and 2nd Earl of Northampton in 1374. Mary (de) Bohun, his younger daughter, became the first wife of Henry IV - see Note 7 also.

6. On Thomas of Woodstocks's death in 1397, his son, Humphrey, became the 2nd Duke of Gloucester and the 2nd Earl of Buckingham. Humphrey died unmarried in 1399, aged 17. Humphrey had four sisters but three died within three years of his death. From her brother, the remaining sister, Anne Plantagenet, was heiress to the earldom of Buckingham and property.

7. From her mother, Eleanor (de) Bohun, who had died in 1399, Anne Plantagenet was heiress to half of the de Bohun estates. The heiress to the other half had been Eleanor's sister, Mary, who, in 1381, had married Henry, Duke of Lancaster, later King Henry IV (r 1399-1413). On Mary's death in 1394, Henry inherited her half share. Mary's son succeeded to the throne as Henry V (r 1413-1422).

8. The office of Lord High Constable had become annexed to the earldom of Hereford and descended through nine generations of the de Bohun family. For more information on the Great Offices of State such as the Lord High Constable, see Appendix 6: Great Offices of State of England.

9. English Dukedoms had been instituted by Edward I as titles for his children. This practice was continued throughout the Middle Ages to reflect, in the main, royal relationships as well as pre-eminent landed wealth.

10. The 1st Duke of Buckingham's holdings in Kent alone, mainly through the Audley inheritance, included Brasted, Dacehurst, Edenbridge, Hadlow, Tonbridge and Yalding. In addition, in 1447, on the death of Humphrey, Duke of Gloucester, he received Penshurst with its magnificent country house and its dependencies. Also, he had control of Dover Castle and the Cinque Ports as well as a large stake in the customs at Sandwich, which, at that time, was England's busiest port.

11. Anne Neville, wife of the 1st Duke of Buckingham, was great aunt to another Anne Neville, who was both the second wife of Richard III and a descendant of Edward III.

12. The Tudor monarchs followed a policy of reducing the independence of the nobility and transforming nobles into courtiers and servants of the Crown restricted to military and ceremonial roles rather than allowing them to exercise any political power.

13. Following the attainder of the 3rd Duke of Buckingham, the hereditary Lord High Constable of England ceased to exist, future Lord High Constables being appointed only for the day of the coronation. See also Appendix 6: Great Offices of State of England.

14. Properties confiscated by the Crown were often distributed to people in favour at the time for consideration of one form or another - for example, money, favours or loyalty. In the case of the 3rd Duke of Buckingham's estates, Penshurst Place eventually went to the Sidney family in 1552, when Edward VI made a gift of it to his loyal steward and tutor, Sir William Sidney. Throughout the turbulent years of Tudor and later, Stuart rule, the Sidneys served at Court and in government. Penshurst's most famous son, Sir Philip Sidney, the chivalrous soldier poet, was a symbol of loyalty and bravery in the Elizabethan era. In total, Henry VIII made no fewer than 72 grants of the Duke's confiscated properties to favoured courtiers, supporters and followers.

15. Mary Stafford, the last of the Staffords, was the sister of Henry Stafford, 5th Lord Stafford.

16. Sir William, later the Blessed William Howard, was the third son of Thomas Howard, 21st Earl of Arundel, who was the grandson of Thomas Howard, 4th Duke of Norfolk. The 4th Duke was implicated in the Ridolfi plot with Philip II of Spain to put Mary, Queen of Scots,

on the English throne and restore Catholicism in England. He was imprisoned in the Tower of London. Subsequently, in 1572, he was beheaded and his titles were forfeited. Thomas Howard, 23rd Earl of Arundel, great great grandson of the 4th Duke, was restored as the 5th Duke of Norfolk in 1660.

17.   The chapter: "What's In A Family Name" provides more information on the Aston/Clifford families.

18.   Inhabitants of the Stafford, the county town of Staffordshire, will be familiar with the name of Blessed William Howard, as it is the name of the town's Roman Catholic secondary school.

19.   The Earldom of Stafford became extinct on the death of the 4th Earl in 1762.

20.   Continuing links with Shropshire and Staffordshire are still in evidence with The Jerningham Arms (which has now been converted into flats), Shifnal, Shropshire, Jerningham Street in Stafford and the Fitzherbert Arms in Swynnerton, close to Swynnerton Hall, the seat of Lord Stafford. For more examples of links to aristocratic families past and present, see Appendix 2: Public Houses, Roads and Place Names.

Titles Move In Mysterious Ways
Acknowledgements

Robinson, John Martin (2002), *The Staffords,* Phillimore & Co; ISBN 1860772196

Staffordshire County Council Education Department

Tom Barley website http://home.it.net.au/%7Ebarleys/stafford.htm (accessed 2004)

Stirnet Limited website http://www.stirnet.com/ (accessed 2004)

Further Reading

Michael Ford - The English Country House - website http://www.britannia.com/history/c-house.html (accessed 2004)

BARONY OF STAFFORD – LINE OF DESCENT

Edmund Stafford
m Anne Plantagenet, grand dau of Edward III
  Humphrey Stafford, 1st Duke of Buckingham (1402-1460) d Battle of Northampton
    Humphrey Stafford, 7th Earl of Stafford (1424-1455) d Battle of St Albans
      Humphrey Stafford, 2nd Duke of Buckingham (1455-1483) exec after unsuccessful rebellion in support of Henry Tudor
        Edward Stafford, 3rd Duke of Buckingham (1478-1521)
          Henry Stafford, 1st Baron Stafford (1501-1547) b Penshurst
            Henry Stafford, 2nd Baron Stafford (1534-1563)
              Edward Stafford, 3rd Baron Stafford (1535-1603)
                Edward Stafford, 4th Baron Stafford (1572-1625)
                  Edward Stafford d 1621
                    Henry Stafford, 5th Baron Stafford
                      Mary Stafford (1619-1694)
                      m William Howard, 1st Viscount Stafford (1612-80 - beheaded), son of 2nd Earl of Arundel
                        John Stafford-Howard (d 1714)
                          Mary Stafford-Howard (d 1765)
                          m Francis Plowden
                            Mary Plowden
                            m Sir George Jerningham, 5th Baronet, (1680-1721) of Costessey, Norfolk
                              Sir William Jerningham, 6th Baronet (1736-1809)
                                Sir George William Jerningham, 7th Baronet and 8th Baron Stafford (1771-1815)
                                Henry Valentine Jerningham, 9th Baron Stafford (1802-84)
                                  Edward Stafford-Jerningham (1804-49)
                                    Augustus Stafford-Jerningham, 10th Baron Stafford (1830-92)
                                    Fitzherbert Edward Stafford-Jerningham, 11th Baron Stafford (1833-1913)
                                    Emily Charlotte Jerningham (1835-81)
                                    m Basil Thomas Fitzherbert (1836-1919)
                                        Francis Edward Fitzherbert, 12th Baron Stafford (1859-1932)
                                          Edward Fitzherbert, 13th Baron Stafford (1864-1941)
                                            Thomas Fitzherbert (1869-1937)
                                              Basil Fitzherbert, 14th Baron Stafford (1926-86)
                                                Francis Fitzherbert, 15th Baron Stafford (1954-)

Note: Roger Stafford, the 1st cousin of Edward, the 4th Baron Stafford should have been the 5th Baron Stafford but was denied the dignity as he was too poor.

Colton's Lost Country House

This chapter is unusual in that the central 'character' is a house and not a person. However, the house in question has close connections with some of the families discussed in other chapters, namely, the Astons and the Howards.

Colton is a small village situated just outside Rugeley, an old market town between Stafford, the county town, and the cathedral city of Lichfield.

However, in earlier times, Colton was a much more important place than its near neighbour, the town of Rugeley.

During the 12th and 13th centuries, Colton's population had grown so much that Colton was considered a town with the largest population between Stafford and Lichfield. In 1235, a Market Charter was granted. Fridays were to be Market Days and the annual fair days were to be held on 8 and 9 September.

In the 14th century, Colton was an important centre of glass making [1] but there are no remains of these centuries, apart from the Church of St Mary.

In the early 17th century, Sir Walter Aston, 1st Lord Aston of Forfar, [2] gave his second son, Herbert, a small estate in Colton. Herbert had acted as his father's secretary in Spain. [3] Herbert's friends and relatives gave or lent money for a new house to be built on the estate. In 1639, Herbert and Catherine Thimelby, the daughter of a Lincolnshire merchant, were married and moved into their new home, which they called Bellamore [4] (Italian for 'good love').

Although Herbert and Catherine were Catholics, in a period when Catholics were mistrusted, they were usually left alone. However, Herbert was caught up in the 'Popish Plot' inspired by Titus Oates and was lucky to escape prison or worse, particularly as Stephen Dugdale [5], one of Oates' accomplices, claimed that the plotters sometimes met at Bellamore.

Herbert died in 1689, in the year following the Glorious Revolution, which brought the Protestants, William and Mary, to the throne, in place of the Catholic James II. Herbert and his son, John, who died in 1724, are buried in unmarked graves somewhere in the churchyard at Colton.

John had no children and Bellamore passed back to the elder branch of the Aston family, in the person of James, the 5th and last Lord Aston. Bellamore then passed to his elder daughter, Mary, who married into the Blount [6] family. Mary (Lady Blount) did not live there whilst her husband, Sir Walter Blount, was alive but, after her husband's death, she frequently resided in Colton.[7]

In about 1795, Lady Blount had a new stone house built for her second son, Edward, who set about laying out the park around the house with shrubberies, trees and a lake. For many years, the 'Old' and 'New' Halls resided alongside one another. The road from Rugeley to Colton was moved further away from the houses, and entrance drives [8] built from the Rugeley and Colwich roads. The farm land was also improved.

In 1823, when the Blounts sold Bellamore, it was described as 'fit for a family of the first consequence'.

The new owner was James Oldham Oldham, a retired Indian judge. Mr Oldham had Bellamour [9] Lodge built for his daughters in 1851. [10]

After Mr Oldham's death in 1857, Bellamour Hall was sold to Thomas Berry Horsfall.[11] Mr Horsfall was a Liverpool merchant, born in Everton in 1805, Mayor of Liverpool in 1848 and Member of Parliament [12] for Liverpool from 1853 to 1868.

Mr Horsfall funded the building of Colton School [13] in 1862 and the Reading Room. He also presented some land adjacent to the school as a new cemetery (now called the Closed Burial Ground) and was one of the founders of the District Hospital in Rugeley, which was converted in the twentieth century into a rest home for the elderly.

Mr Horsfall was married four times - his fourth wife, Lucy, was 41 years younger than him. Lucy had four daughters, all of whom lived at Colton and died unmarried. Mr Horsfall died in 1878, Lucy in 1920 and his youngest daughter in 1957. His wife and daughter are buried in the Closed Burial Ground along with some other members of the Horsfall family.

Lucy left the Bellamour Hall Estate to a relative, Henry Leeke Horsfall, who put it up for sale by auction on 4 June 1921. The sale took place at the Swan Hotel, Stafford.[14]

After this time, the Bellamour estate faded into obscurity. Bellamour (New) Hall is reported to have been demolished around 1930. [15, 16] There is also some unverified documentation that it burnt down in about 1930 after having been left empty for some years. [17]

This was a rather sad end to an estate, which had an interesting brush with British national history.

Colton's Lost Country House
Further Notes and Connections

1. Evidence of glassmaking has also been found in the Wolseley area, which is only a short distance from Colton. For more on the Wolseleys, see the chapter: "This Land Was My Land".

2. There is some evidence that Walter, 1st Lord Aston of Forfar, had a clandestine marriage, to one Anne Barnes, which was dissolved in 1600, Anne Barnes having been committed to the Fleet Prison. The only marriage recorded in most documents is that to Gertrude Sadleir, daughter of Sir Thomas Sadleir of Standon, Hertfordshire. The 1st Lord Aston's grandfather, another Sir Walter Aston, married Elizabeth Leveson, daughter of Sir James Leveson around 1545. For more on the Levesons/Leveson-Gowers, see the chapter: "A Family Of Influence". Sir Walter's son, Edward, married twice, his first marriage being to Mary Spencer, daughter of Sir John Spencer of Althorp, a member of the family of the late Diana, Princess of Wales.

3. As noted in the chapter: "What's In A Family Name", Sir Walter Aston was sent to Spain as Ambassador from 1620 - 1625 to try and arrange a marriage between the Infanta daughter of Philip III, and Charles, Prince of Wales. On his second visit from 1635 - 1638 he became a Roman Catholic. He was created the 1st Lord Aston of Forfar on 28 November 1627. He has an extensive biography in the Dictionary of National Biography published by the Oxford University Press.

4. The Italian spelling 'Bellamore' remained in use from 1639 until, probably, the early/mid 19th century before being superseded by the French spelling 'Bellamour'. See Note 7.

5. Stephen Dugdale had been the steward at Tixall Hall, the home of Herbert's father, the first Lord Aston.

6. It is said that the Blounts can be traced back to three brothers who came over with William the Conqueror and that Sir Walter was descended from the Norman Lord of Guisnes, surnamed 'Le Blond'. He also numbered amongst his ancestors the 'warlike Blount' celebrated by Shakespeare in his Henry IV. See also the chapter: "What's In A Family Name?" The name is normally pronounced 'Blunt'. Sir Walter's family lived at Mawley Hall, near Cleobury Mortimer. Staffordshire Blounts

also lived at Blount's Hall near Uttoxeter, and Penkridge. An area on the outskirts of Uttoxeter is still called Blount's Green. For further information on the Blounts, see Appendix 5: The Blounts.

7. Lady Blount was burned to death in 1805 by a spark falling on her dress when on a visit to her youngest son's house at Basford, now a suburb of Stoke-on-Trent.

8. As at 2005, the two former entrance lodges to Bellamour Hall still existed, although both had been substantially altered and added to.

9. By the 1850s, the present French-style spelling of Bellamour had come into use.

10. One of James Oldham's daughters, Ellen, ran a day school for girls in Bellamour Old Hall from 1829. She continued to live in Bellamour Lodge until she died in 1883. Her sister, who married Mr John Thomas Harland, also lived at Bellamour Lodge for most of her life. In 1884, Mrs Harland had eight almshouses erected in memory of her sister. My grandmother, Linda May Upton (née Bloom), who had been in service at Bellamour Lodge in her younger days, spent her final years in one of these almshouses.

11. Thomas Berry Horsfall had an interesting background, which may have influenced his support of the American Confederates. His father, Charles Horsfall, who was born in Huddersfield in 1776, married Dorothy Hall Berry in Liverpool on 9 June 1803. Dorothy, the daughter of Thomas Berry and Dorothy Hall, was born and baptised in Jamaica in October 1784.

12. During the American Civil War (1861 - 1865), T B Horsfall was one of many Members of Parliament, who purchased cotton bonds from the Confederate government in the hope of securing recognition of the fledgling nation so they could 'cash in' their war bonds for cotton. Unfortunately for the South, they did not attract enough British investors to convince Her Majesty's Government to intervene on the side of the Confederacy.

13. Both my mother, Sybil Mary Sproston (née Upton) and I attended Colton School and experienced the same headmaster, Ernest Broughton.

14. The sale of the Bellamour Hall Estate was conducted by Winterton & Sons of St Mary's Chambers, Lichfield. According to their sale catalogue, the estate comprised 391½ acres with the following being offered for sale: The Manor or Reputed Manor of Colton; Bellamour Hall and two Entrance Lodges, extensive Pleasure Grounds, Lawns and Ornamental Water and Boat House; Home Farm and Plantations;

Colton House, Parchfields; New House Farm; several Small Holdings; Dwelling Houses and Accommodation Lands in or near Colton. According to an annotated copy of the sale catalogue in the possession of the William Salt Library, not all the lots were sold - Colton House was withdrawn but Parchfields was sold for £2,700. The fact that Henry Leeke Horsfall continued to be described as Lord of the Manor until as late as 1940 suggests a substantial part of the estate was unsold.

15. Ironically, Bellamour Old Hall lasted quite a few years longer, although derelict. Some ruins still remained in 1969 when a survey was carried out by the Department of the Environment.

16. An article in The Rugeley Times of 15 July 1967 states that stone from Bellamour Hall was reputedly taken to America so that a replica of an English stately home could be built there. My father, John Sproston, who was born in 1920 at Wolseley Bridge, remembers hearing a similar story when he was young. There was a similar story in The Rugeley Times of 19 February 1972, which probably used the previous newspaper article as its source. No primary confirmation source has been identified to date.

17. There is also a nostalgic reference to Bellamour Hall in an article, entitled Random Notes, in the Staffordshire Advertiser of 14 September 1935: "Whenever, I visit the Colton district, I feel a pang of regret because of the departed glories of Bellamour Hall, and, when I was in the locality several days ago, I felt strong hopes that Bellamour Lodge would not travel the same way towards demolition". In the same newspaper, details were given of the sale of Bellamour Lodge the previous Thursday night. The sale by public auction was carried out at the Shrewsbury Arms Hotel, Rugeley, by Messrs Barber & Son of Stafford and Wellington. Bidding started at £1,000 and advanced steadily until it was sold at £1,500. Bellamour Lodge was described as an attractive Georgian residence with stabling, gardens and grounds. Bellamour Lodge still exists today.

Colton's Lost Country House
Acknowledgements

Colton - Staffordshire County Council - ISSN 03065820

William Salt Library, Stafford

- Messrs Winterton & Sons - Sales Catalogue - 4 June 1921

-The Staffordshire Advertiser, Saturday, 14 September 1935

The Rugeley Times

Comrades in Bonds: The Subsidized Sale of Confederate War Debt to British Leaders - Marc D. Weidenmier, Claremont McKenna College and NBER February 2003 website

http://www.stanford.edu/group/sshi/Conferences/2002-2003/Debt2003/weidenmier.pdf#search='weidenmier%20Comrades%20in%20Bonds' (accessed 2004)

Dr David Paterson - The Halls of Jamaica website

http://www.clanphail.org/UFT/html/JAMAICA/ (accessed 2004)

Further Reading

Felbridge & District History Group website (Blount connection with Bellamour)

http://www.jeremy-clarke.freeserve.co.uk/handouts/Imberhorne.htm (accessed 2004)

From Tree Lover to Restaurateur

Over the years, Staffordshire has suffered from a lot of bad press, much of it unjustified.

In some cases, either through ignorance, or not wishing to accept the truth, Staffordshire has not had the recognition it deserves.

The 'Derbyshire' Peak District is one example of this apparent desire to wipe Staffordshire from the map of desirable areas to visit. Even the Derbyshire website: http://www.derbyshireuk.net/townsandvillages.html lists several villages under the heading 'Towns and villages in Derbyshire', which are most definitely in Staffordshire, including Alstonefield, Flash, Grindon, Warslow and Wetton! In fact, some of the best parts of the so-called Derbyshire Peak District are actually in Staffordshire, for example, the Roaches and part of Dovedale .[1]

Another example is Weston Park [2] at Weston-under-Lizard.[3] Although the Shropshire border crosses the A5 just a few hundred yards west of Weston Park and passes through the estate, the main house at Weston Park is most definitely in Staffordshire.

The current house at Weston Park was completed in 1671 and was built on the site of an earlier mediaeval manor house. This house is a wonderful legacy of Lady Wilbraham (née Elizabeth Mytton), a forebear of the current (7th) Earl of Bradford.

Weston Park has belonged to the Earl of Bradford's family and its forebears since the twelfth century with ownership passing through both male and female lines. At the time of the Domesday Book, Weston was held by Rainald de Balgiole (Bailleuil), Sheriff to Roger de Montgomery, Earl of Shrewsbury. Thereafter, the de Westons were in possession until 1350 when a co-heiress married Sir Adam de Peshall.[4] Their great grandson, another Sir Adam de Peshall, had two heiresses, one of whom, Margaret, married Sir Richard (de) Mytton, and conveyed to him the Weston-under-Lizard estate.[5]

Sir Richard's descendant, Edward Mytton, whose grandfather, Edward

Harpsfield, took the name of Mytton on succeeding to the property under the will of his maternal grandfather, John Mytton, who died in 1532. Edward (Harpsfield) Mytton's daughter, Elizabeth, married Sir Thomas Wilbraham, Baronet, of Woodhey, Cheshire. They had one daughter, Cecilia, who died in infancy and three daughters, Elizabeth [6], Grace [7] and Mary, who all survived to adulthood. Mary, who was the heiress to Weston, married Richard Newport, 2nd Earl of Bradford (First Creation).[8,9] They had two sons, Henry (3rd Earl) and Thomas (4th and last Earl of the first creation) and two daughters, Diana, who married the 6th Earl of Mountrath, and Anne, who married Sir Orlando Bridgeman [10], 4th Baronet, of Castle Bromwich Hall, near Birmingham. Following a deed of partition, Anne's son, Sir Henry Bridgeman, 5th Baronet, inherited Weston, which became the main Bridgeman seat - Castle Bromwich Hall was let out to tenants. Sir Henry's son, another Orlando, became the 1st Earl of Bradford (of the Second Creation).

Since then, descent has passed directly through the male line to Richard, born in 1947, who succeeded as the 7th Earl on the death of his father, the 6th Earl, in 1981. The 7th Earl is well known as a restaurateur - in 1979, he opened 'Porters English Restaurant', which was aimed at filling a gap that existed in the market for reasonably priced real English food.[11]

On his father's death he faced a tax bill of £8 million, which forced him to dispose of all his London interests, apart from Porters, and concentrate on paying off this huge sum. This task was eventually accomplished in 1986, with help from the National Heritage Memorial Fund, which resulted in Weston Park being put into a Charitable Foundation.

Gerald, the 6th Earl, who succeeded to the title in 1957, was a highly respected and self-taught expert on trees and forestry. He was responsible for the planting of many trees on the Weston estate and, for many years, was a Crown Estate Commissioner.

As noted earlier, one of the forebear families of the present Earls of Bradford were the Myttons. There is some documentary evidence that these Myttons were related to John Mytton, who has been called the "maddest squire in England". John Mytton was descended from Reginald de Mutton, a Norman nobleman, whose descendants were prominent in Shropshire for many generations. John Mytton must be one of the most eccentric men who have ever lived - he was only 38 when he died, having, by some accounts, not been sober for a single day since he was 15. In that time, he had spent a huge fortune on drink, horses (a great love of his), hunting and clothes as well as giving away large sums of money. Practical jokes and daredevil escapades made life worth living for John Mytton.

From Tree Lover To Restaurateur
Further Notes and Connections

1. John Hillaby in his book "Journey through Britain" claims that Staffordshire deserves more credit than it usually gets noting that people forget about Cannock Chase and that some of the best dales scenery lies within Staffordshire in an area, which many people think of as the Derbyshire Peak District. For more on this area, see also the next chapter: "The North Staffordshire Wallabies".

2. It has been claimed that Weston Park is the setting of Blandings Castle, the setting for several of the stories written by P G Wodehouse. Miss Fallowfield's Fortune (1908), a novel written by Ellen Thorneycroft Fowler, is mainly set in Weston-under-Lizard and Weston Park.

3. Weston under Lizard derives its name from the neighbouring Lizard Hill in Shropshire. 'Lizard' is a corruption of 'Lazar's Yard', i.e. a leper colony. The Order of Saint Lazarus was founded in the 12th century to provide nursing for lepers, taking Lazarus as its patron. The knights of the order were lepers, and besides helping their fellow sufferers, they carried out military duties. They founded a hospital for lepers near the northern wall of Jerusalem. Consequently, many leper colonies were named after St Lazarus, who was the poor man at the gate of the rich man in Christ's parable related in St Luke's Gospel.

4. Sir Adam de Peshall (sometimes spelt Pershall) married a second time to another heiress, the daughter of John de Caverswall of Bishop's Offley (mid-Staffordshire).

5. Margaret de Peshall's sister, Johanna, married a member of the de Bermingham family, who controlled the area around Birmingham from the late 11th century until 1527, when John Dudley, Duke of Northumberland, gained control.

6. Elizabeth Wilbraham married Sir Thomas Middleton (sometimes spelt Myddleton) of Chirk Castle, which he bought in 1595, and who was Lord Mayor of London in 1613. After Elizabeth died in childbirth, Sir Thomas married Charlotte Bridgeman, the daughter of Sir Orlando Bridgeman, Lord Keeper of the Great Seal - see Note 10 below. Sir Thomas therefore had two connections with forebears of the current Earls of Bradford - the Wilbrahams and the Bridgemans.

7. Grace Wilbraham, who was the heiress of Woodhey and Peckforton in Cheshire, married Lionel Tollemache, Lord Huntingtour and 2nd Earl of Dysart. A portrait of Grace hangs in the Marble Hall of the mansion house at Weston Park.

8. The Bradford of the Earldom of Bradford relates to the North and South Hundreds of Bradford in Shropshire.

9. Richard Newport's grandfather, also named Richard, had been created Baron Newport by Charles I in 1642 as he marched through Stafford. Sir Richard paid £6,000 to purchase the title. The first Lord Newport married Rachel Leveson, daughter of Sir John Leveson of Haling, Kent, and Lilleshall, Shropshire. For more on the Leveson family - see the chapter: "A Family Of Influence".

10. Sir Orlando Bridgeman, 1608-74, great-great-great grandfather of the 1st Earl of Bradford of the second creation, was the son of a clergyman, who became Bishop of Chester. An eminent lawyer, Sir Orlando presided over the trial of the regicides in 1660 following the restoration of Charles II. However, he was dismissed in 1672 after he obstructed the passage of grants, which Charles II wished to make to his mistresses as well as attacking the commission for martial law and opposing the 'Stop of the Exchequer', which allowed Charles to default on Crown debts. This act came about when goldsmiths refused to lend more money to the king who had already borrowed huge sums. He therefore prohibited most payments from the Exchequer, initially for a year and later indefinitely. In the late 1670s and the 1680s, several of his largest creditors went bankrupt. During the mid-1600s, the practice had developed among some goldsmiths of dealing in foreign and domestic coins and letting their safes be used for deposits of valuables - this was a natural progression to their becoming bankers. On Sir Orlando's removal from his position as Lord Keeper of the Great Seal, he melted down the seal rather than returning it.

11. The 7th Earl has also written a book called 'Stately Secrets', which is a compilation of amusing anecdotes about members of the aristocracy and their servants - see Further Reading below.

From Tree Lover To Restaurateur
Acknowledgements

Davies, Glyn , rev. ed. (1996), *A History of Money from Ancient Times to the Present Day,* Cardiff: University of Wales Press; ISBN 0708313515

Lakeland, Christine - compiler (1987), *Weston Park,* English Life Publications Ltd; ISBN 0851012582

Quinn, Tom (1996), *Tales of the Country Eccentrics,* David & Charles; ISBN 0715303473

Further Reading

Bridgeman, Richard Thomas Orlando - Earl of Bradford (1995), *Stately Secrets: Behind-the-scenes Stories from the Stately Homes of Britain,* Robson Books Ltd; ISBN 0860519171

Hillaby, John (1968), *Journey through Britain,* Constable, ISBN 0094557802

The North Staffordshire Wallabies

In the early part of the 21st century, there were newspaper reports that, the wallabies, which had been roaming the North Staffordshire countryside around the Roaches for around 50 years, had finally died out - the last one is believed to have been sighted in 2001.

These wallabies originated from the Brocklehurst family estate, the most famous of this family being Philip Lee Brocklehurst, who was born at Swythamley Park, Staffordshire, on 7 March 1887, and became the second baronet in 1904. In 1906, while an undergraduate at Trinity Hall, Cambridge, he met Ernest Henry Shackleton and the following year joined the British Antarctic Expedition, 1907-1909 (led by Shackleton), as assistant geologist. This expedition is sometimes known as the Nimrod Expedition after the ship they sailed in. It is also believed that Sir Philip's mother part-funded the expedition.

Badly frostbitten feet prevented Sir Philip from making the first ascent of Mount Erebus, still an active volcano. Nevertheless, the subsequent amputation of his big toe did not prevent him from participating in several other journeys exploring the Taylor Valley and Ferrar Glacier.

Enlisting in the Derbyshire Imperial Yeomanry, Sir Philip served with the First Life Guards during the First World War, and between 1918 and 1920, with the Egyptian Army. In 1924, he was made a brevet lieutenant colonel. During the Second World War, he commanded the Second Regiment Arab Legion Merchandised Brigade and, from 1943 to 1944, served with the British Council in Palestine-Trans-Jordan. After the war, he returned to Staffordshire to look after his estate.

He died on 28 January 1975, the last survivor of Shackleton's British Antarctic Expedition mentioned above.

The history of Swythamley Park is quite well documented in old deeds and other documents.[1] It is stated that Hugh de Meschines, 5th Earl of Chester, died here at his hunting seat in 1180. In 1221, the 6th Earl of Chester, Ranulph de Blondeville, as an act of piety on returning from the Crusade, built the Abbey of Dieulacres, a few miles away near Leek. He then endowed the Abbey with his manor and forests at Swythamley. The Abbey then held Swythamley Park until 1538, when it was seized as part of the Dissolution of the Monasteries. Henry VIII then granted it to his close friend, William Trafford.

The Trafford family owned the estate until it was sold in 1831 to William Brocklehurst [2], a silk manufacture. His nephew, Philip Lancaster Brocklehurst [2], inherited it in 1859, later becoming the first Brocklehurst Baronet. He died in 1904 leaving a young wife, who lived at the Bagstones, Wincle, until about 1950, and a young family of two sons and a daughter. His elder son, Philip Lee Brocklehurst, the second Baronet, had a long and colourful life. As well as being a member of the British Antarctic Expedition, noted earlier, which was partly financed by his mother, he was also the first man to cross the Sahara Desert by motor car in the 1920s. Together with his brother, (Henry) Courtney Brocklehurst, who had been a game warden in the Sudan, he went on many hunting trips to Africa and Asia bringing back many animal heads as trophies. These used to be displayed in the tenants' hall at the estate.

Although, sadly, Courtney Brocklehurst was drowned during World War II in Burma, Sir Philip lived until 1975. After his death [3], the estate with its 40 or so farms and cottages was sold. The main house and park became a centre for transcendental meditation for about 10 years and was then sold to a developer, who split the house and buildings into about 8 separate units. The estate church is also now a house. The park, however, is very much at it was in the 1800s with its huge boundary wall about a mile long and the south and west gates and lodges still in place.

Courtney had lived at Roaches Hall, a former Victorian hunting lodge, built in 1876 by his father, Sir Philip Brocklehurst, with stone from local quarries. Courtney amassed a small zoo in the grounds including yaks, llamas, deer and wallabies. These were later let loose on the Roaches, gradually dying off until only the deer and the wallabies were left. The deer were poached out of existence and, as stated earlier, it is believed that the wallabies may have died out around 2001.

Roaches Hall is close to The Roaches [4], which with Hen Cloud and Ramshaw Rocks, form a gritstone escarpment marking the south-western edge of the Peak District. Best viewed from the approach along the Leek road, they stand as a line of silent sentinels guarding the entrance to the Peak District, worn into fantastic shapes by the elements.

Following the break up of the Swythamley Estate, the area including the Roaches and Hen Cloud (an area of 975 acres) was purchased in 1980 by the Peak National Park in order to protect this unique area and guarantee access for the public.

Hen Cloud is an impressive, solitary edge, which rises steeply from the ground below. The Roaches themselves have a gentler approach and actually consist of two edges, a Lower and Upper tier, with a set of rock-steps connecting them.

Built into the rocks of the Lower Tier is Rock Cottage, a tiny primitive cottage, which was once the gamekeeper's residence and has now been converted into a climbing hut. Below and to the west of the main edge is a line of small subsidiary edges known as the Five Clouds.

The whole area is a favourite place with walkers and rock-climbers, and the edges provide some of the best gritstone climbing in the country, with famous classic routes such as Valkyrie, the Sloth and The Swan.

In some ways the area has become a victim of its own popularity for the area is very busy at weekends.

The North Staffordshire Wallabies
Further Notes and Connections

1. Swythamley has also been identified as the probable site of the castle of the Green Knight of the classic mediaeval poem 'Sir Gawain and the Green Knight' and nearby Lud's Church as the knight's 'Green Chapel'. It is therefore likely that the unknown author was connected with the Abbey of Dieulacres. Lud's Church is not a church but a fantastic gorge, 60ft deep and barely eight feet wide. The name comes from the Lollards, a group of mediaeval heretics, and followers of John Wycliffe, who were led by Sir Walter de Lud Auk. Fearing the usual treatment meted out to heretics, they gathered here to avoid the enthusiastic stake burners and it is easy to imagine this mossy, sodden and fern-smothered enclosure offering a hidden refuge for those on the fringe of the law. See Appendix 7: Dissolution of the Monasteries and the Reformation for further notes on the Lollards and Dieulacres Abbey.

2. The Brocklehursts were related to the Dent-Brocklehursts of Sudeley Castle in Gloucestershire - Emma Dent, née Brocklehurst, was Sir Philip Lee Brocklehurst's aunt. In 2004, there was an exhibition of Sir Philip's Antarctic Adventure at Sudeley Castle.

3. Sir Philip Lancaster Brocklehurst, the 1st baronet, is buried in a crypt under the family chapel along with his wife, daughter and a servant. This chapel, which was built in 1904 in the grounds of the Swythamley estate, is now a private home.

4. John Ogilvy Brocklehurst, son of (Henry) Courtney Brocklehurst and Lady Helen Alice Wyllington Ogilvy, became the 3rd (and last) baronet after the death of his uncle, Sir Philip Lee Brocklehurst. Lady Helen was daughter of the 6th Earl of Airlie. Sir John died in 1981.

5. The Roaches were used as the backdrop for the moor scenes in the definitive version of Arthur Conan Doyle's 'The Hound of the Baskervilles' starring Jeremy Brett as Sherlock Holmes. Another North Staffordshire location, Heath House, was used as the setting for Baskerville Hall in the same film. Heath House, a fine 19th century mansion, lies about a mile from the centre of Upper Tean, near Cheadle, Staffordshire, on the road towards Hollington.

The North Staffordshire Wallabies
Acknowledgements

Staffordshire Moorlands District Council website: www.staffsmoorlands.gov. uk (accessed 2004)

Cressbrook Multimedia website: www.cressbrook.co.uk/leek/roaches.htm et al (accessed 2004/05)

Further Reading

Brocklehurst, Sir Philip (1998), *Swythamley and Its Neighbourhood Past and Present,* Churnet Valley Books; ISBN 1902685016

The Happy Valley Connection

In December 1942, Sir John Henry 'Jock' Delves Broughton, the 11th Baronet, committed suicide at the Adelphi Hotel in Liverpool only a few months after returning from the Wanjohi Valley (known for posterity as 'Happy Valley') north of Nairobi in Kenya. So ended a scandalous life but not the end of the story - in 1987, the film 'White Mischief' was released. This film, starring Greta Scacchi, Joss Ackland and Charles Dance, was based on the murder of Lord Erroll in the Happy Valley and its aftermath.

Sir Jock inherited substantial wealth on becoming the 11th Baronet. This inheritance did not include Broughton Hall, [1] near Eccleshall, a few miles from the county town of Stafford; the hall had been sold to a Mr John Hall sometime between 1914 and 1917.

By the mid 1930s, Sir Jock was in financial difficulties, which resulted in his taking some desperate measures. First, he sold a large part of the family's landholdings in Cheshire, which, in fact, were held in trust and, therefore, not his to sell. Next, he claimed and received insurance money following the theft of three valuable paintings and some pearls despite the suspicions of the insurers and the police. However, they were unable to prove that any fraud had taken place.

After his first wife left him for Lord Moyne [2], Sir Jock and his second wife, Diana (née Caldwell) [3] left the UK in November 1940 and went to live in the 'Happy Valley' in Kenya. There they met Josslyn Hay, 22nd Earl of Erroll, and Hereditary Lord High Constable of Scotland. [4,5] Lord Erroll was the uncrowned king of the Happy Valley set - a hard-drinking, philandering rake, who took great pleasure in cuckolding his male friends. It was the notorious antics of Lord Erroll and his glamorous titled friends in Kenya's White Highlands that led to the joke whereby members of British society would be asked: "Are you married, or do you live in Kenya?" [6]

The discovery of Lord Erroll's bullet-ridden body on the outskirts of Nairobi on 24 January 1941 and the subsequent court case made headlines around the world. There were many suspects. However, the substantial circumstantial evidence, which has accumulated, points to Sir Jock Delves Broughton being the most likely murderer - although he stood trial for the murder and was acquitted, this was on a technicality and he committed suicide a year later. In addition, Juanita Carberry, author of 'Child of Happy Valley', who was a 15-year-old schoolgirl living in Kenya at the time, claims that Sir Jock confessed to her shortly after the murder when he met her in her parents' stables.

After the film, it is likely that the affair would have faded into obscurity but for the intervention of Errol Trzebinski, a local historian. In her book 'The Life and Death of Lord Erroll', she claims that Lord Erroll was the victim of an SOE plot – Lord Erroll was said to have links with the British Fascist movement.

The Happy Valley Connection
Further Notes and Connections

1.   During World War II (1939 - 1945), two schools were evacuated to Broughton Hall. The pupils included two future Conservative MPs: Michael Heseltine and Julian Critchley.

2.   Lord Moyne was born Walter Edward Guinness, the 3rd son of the 1st Earl of Iveagh, the head of the Guinness brewing family. In August 1942, Lord Moyne was assassinated in Cairo by members of a Zionist terrorist group, the Stern Gang. This premeditated murder was meant to send a clear message directly to the highest echelons of the alleged pro-Arab British Foreign Office. His elder son, the 2nd Lord Moyne, was the author Bryan Guinness, who married Diana Mitford in 1929. They were divorced in 1933, following which Diana married Sir Oswald Mosley, the founder of the British Union of Fascists. Mosley's family were prosperous landowners in Staffordshire. One of Diana's sisters, Deborah, known as Debo, is the current Dowager Duchess of Devonshire (as of early 2007).

3.   As at early 2007, the owner of Broughton Hall was the well-known North Staffordshire mobile phone entrepreneur, John Caudwell.

4.   The Lord High Constable of Scotland was originally one of the great officers of state to which was attached numerous duties and privileges. In early times, he had precedence next to the Lord High Chancellor but from the reign of James VI of Scotland (James I of England), the Lord High Treasurer took precedence. In the royal army, the Lord High Constable was supreme officer next to the King. He was also the supreme judge in all matters of riot, disorder, bloodshed and murder committed within a circuit of four miles of the King's person.

5.   See also Appendix 6: Great Offices of State of England. Many illustrious people have held these posts including one or more of the families with Staffordshire connections, some of which are covered in this book.

6.   See also the chapter: "The Lord Who Nearly Prevented World War 2" for another anecdote on the attitudes of the white inhabitants of Happy Valley.

The Happy Valley Connection
Acknowledgements

Cockin, Tim, *The Staffordshire Encyclopaedia,* Malthouse Press; ISBN 0953901807

Further Reading

Trzebinski, Errol (2000), *The Life and Death of Lord Erroll: The Truth Behind The Happy Valley Murder*, Fourth Estate Ltd; ISBN 1857028945

The Premier Earls

The Earls of Shrewsbury held a very powerful position in England for a long period of time. As descendants of supporters of William the Conqueror, the Shrewsbury families were major landowners, with properties throughout England, which they further consolidated through marriage and the Dissolution of the Monasteries. [1]

The Earldom of Shrewsbury and Waterford is the premier earldom of the United Kingdom and dates back to 1442, when Sir John Talbot was created the Earl of the County of Salop, or, as usually styled, the Earl of Shrewsbury. He took this title from his maternal estates in Shropshire, inherited from the Le Stranges of Blackmere, near Whitchurch.[2] He inherited, on the death of Gilbert, his elder brother, the Talbot estates of Goodrich Castle [3] in Herefordshire, property on the Welsh borders and elsewhere. In 1446, he was also created the first Earl of Waterford.

The 1st Earl was killed on 17 July 1453, along with his son, John, 1st Viscount Lisle [4], at Castillon, which is situated on the Dordogne east of Bordeaux in France. The Battle of Castillon is regarded as the final engagement of The Hundred Years' War [5] leaving Calais as the only English foothold in France. There is a column marking the site where the 1st Earl fell near to the river. It is on the spot where a chapel, 'Notre Dame de Talbot' had been erected by the French soon after the battle - later to be called 'La Tombe de Talbot' and then destroyed during the French Revolution. Over time, the 1st Earl's remains were moved. First, all the remains but the skull were reburied in Falaise. Later, his skull was removed to England, followed by the rest of his remains in 1493. His final burial place was at Whitchurch, Shropshire. It is said that his name spread terror among the French and children were scared into obedience for fear that 'the Talbot cometh'. He has been described as 'an aggressive and combative nobleman, whose energies were best employed abroad if domestic peace was to be preserved'. [6] His main tactics were surprise attacks - he regularly appeared where least expected.

Prior to becoming the 1st Earl of Shrewsbury, John had become the first Talbot Lord of Sheffield and Hallamshire in right of his first wife Maud (de) Nevill(e), the Lady Furnival(l).

John, the 2nd Earl, who was Lord Treasurer, was killed during the Wars of the Roses at the Battle of Northampton in 1460, fighting for the Lancastrian cause. He was buried at Worksop Priory in Nottinghamshire. John, the 3rd Earl, married Catherine Stafford, daughter of Humphrey Stafford, 1st Duke of Buckingham.[7] The 4th to 8th Earls are descended from the 3rd Earl. The 9th to present day Earls are descended from the 3rd Earl's brother, Sir Gilbert via Gilbert's son, Sir John, as shown in the abbreviated family trees, which follow.

George, the 4th Earl, born in Shropshire, and Francis, the 5th Earl, were both prominent at the early Tudor Courts. Francis benefited from the Dissolution of the Monasteries with large grants of monastic and chantry lands, notably Rufford Abbey, Worksop Priory, Glossop and Rotherham. Worksop Priory was granted to Francis on condition that he and his successors as Lords of the Manor of Worksop provided a fine glove for the right hand of the Sovereign at the Coronation and supported the Sovereign's right arm on that day as long as it should hold the sceptre - an obligation still in force today.

Ingestre Hall [8,9], near Stafford, and Alton Towers [10], near Cheadle, Staffordshire, are two other properties that the Shrewsbury family once owned over the centuries.[11]

George, the 6th Earl, has two claims to fame - as the long-time custodian/jailer of Mary, Queen of Scots from 1569 to 1584, and as one of the husbands of Bess of Hardwick.[12] George used his immense inherited wealth to become what would today be called a tycoon, probably one of the greatest of his day. He had large estates in at least seven counties [13], developed coalmines and glassworks, carried out lead and iron smelting in Derbyshire and Herefordshire and was an ironmaster and shipowner. However, this fortune was depleted by the unenviable task of being the warder of Mary, Queen of Scots.[14] Nonetheless, he made various settlements to provide landed estates for his younger sons and dowers for his daughters. For example, the Rufford estate passed to his daughter, Mary, who married Sir George Savile.

George's son, Gilbert, the 7th Earl, had three daughters and co-heiresses. Alathea, the youngest, married Thomas Howard, 21st Earl of Arundel. All subsequent Dukes of Norfolk are descended from her. The Dukes of Norfolk also inherited the old Talbot titles of Barons Talbot, Strange and Furnival, until these fell into abeyance on the death of the 9th Duke of Norfolk. Thomas and Alathea's third son was William Howard, Viscount Stafford.[15] When the 7th

Earl of Shrewsbury died in 1616, the earldom passed to his brother, Edward, who died in the following year. As Edward had no male heir, the earldom passed to a more distant relative, his fourth cousin, George Talbot. George, the 9th Earl, [16] was the great great grandson of Gilbert Talbot, a brother of the 3rd Earl of Shrewsbury.

Charles Talbot, the 12th Earl of Shrewsbury, was also created the first (and only) Duke of Shrewsbury. He was one of the 'Immortal Seven' [17] who signed the letter of invitation to William of Orange, the future William III. Later, in 1714, he was influential in bringing about the peaceful accession of George I, the Elector of Hanover, following the death of Queen Anne. Charles, who was brought up as a Catholic, had converted to the Anglican faith in 1679. His first cousin, Gilbert, succeeded him as the 13th Earl.

It was Charles, the 15th Earl, who began to take more interest in the Alton estate than his predecessors. In 1806/07, around 13,000 trees, conifers and deciduous, were planted in the grounds and major work on the house began in 1811. His nephew, John, the 16th Earl, took over work with the same enthusiasm.

John and his first cousin, Bertram, the 17th Earl, are well known for their association with Augustus Welby Northmore Pugin, the celebrated 19th century architect and designer, who was a Roman Catholic convert. Funded by the immense wealth of the 16th Earl and the fervour often associated with a religious convert of any persuasion, Pugin was able to design and have erected, during the period 1836 -1848, numerous buildings in Staffordshire including St Mary's, Uttoxeter; the Hospital of St John, Alton Castle and Alton Towers; St Giles' Church, School and Presbytery; St Joseph's Convent, also in Cheadle; St Wilfrid's, Cotton; St Mary's, Brewood. St Giles' Church, Cheadle, is considered to be the finest of all of Pugin's churches with the interior being particularly impressive. It is not surprising that St Giles' is known as 'Pugin's Gem', a soubriquet said to have been first applied by the 18th Earl, himself. But even such a wonderful building can elicit very different views; to some people, it is a monument to aristocratic eccentricity; to others, it is an ostentatious demonstration of wealth.

It will have already been noted by the reader that the succession to the Shrewsbury earldom has often not been a simple father to son affair but has frequently hopped around. As noted earlier, the 12th Earl became the first and last Duke of Shrewsbury. On his death, the earldom passed to his first cousin,

Gilbert, and, on his death, the title was inherited by Gilbert's nephew, George Talbot. Then there were the succession hops from the 15th Earl to the 17th Earl - uncle to nephew to cousin. However, these were relatively minor hops compared with the leap from the 17th Earl to the 18th Earl. Bertram Arthur Talbot (1832 - 1856), the 17th Earl, died unmarried as a young man. He believed himself to be the last descendant in the male line of the 1st Earl and consequently had willed his extensive property to a son of the Duke of Norfolk. However, a male Talbot heir did in fact exist, his very distant kinsman, his 8th cousin: Henry John Chetwynd-Talbot, 3rd Earl Talbot of Hensol. Nonetheless, it was not until 1858 that the Committee of Privileges in the British Parliament allowed Henry's claim to the earldom as the 18th Earl. When the 18th Earl died, he was succeeded by his eldest son, Charles John Chetwynd-Talbot (1830 - 1877), the 19th Earl. This was the first time in over 200 years, since the death of the 11th Earl in 1667, that the title of Earl of Shrewsbury had passed from father to son.

Henry, the 18th Earl, had an eventful naval career - he entered the Royal Navy in 1817; became a Lieutenant in 1824; Commander in 1826; Captain in 1827 (the result of his distinguished command of the 'Philomel' at the battle of Navarino, 20 October, 1827); Rear-Admiral in 1854; Vice Admiral in 1865: and finally Admiral in 1865.[18] He was also Member of Parliament for South Staffordshire from 1837 until 1849, and Naval ADC to Queen Victoria (1852 - 54). As Hereditary High Steward of Ireland, he took part in the installation of the Prince of Wales as a K.P. [19] at St. Patrick's Cathedral, Dublin, in 1868.

The 20th Earl, Charles Henry John Chetwynd-Talbot, financed the setting up of Clément Talbot Limited, initially to import the French Clément car into the UK. Manufacture in the UK started later. A Talbot car was the first motor vehicle to travel 100 miles in an hour.

The 21st Earl and his wife, Nadine (née Crofton) were the subject of much media attraction in the late 1950s. In 1954, at the age of 41, after producing six children, Nadine made her debut as a soprano, under the name of Nadine Talbot, in a recital at London's Wigmore Hall. Besides being an accomplished operatic singer and a stylish hostess, she had for many years appeared to the outside world as an advertisement for domestic happiness. But this facade was destroyed in 1959 when the earl sued for divorce on the grounds of Nadine's alleged adultery with Anthony Lowther, the earl's former private secretary. At the time, Lowther was 27 and the Countess 45. Although the judge found the case proved, both Lowther and the Countess strenuously continued to deny that any affair had taken place. Moreover, the judge had a surprise for the earl - he decided that Lady Shrewsbury's conduct did not explain the earl's own admitted adultery with Nina Mortlock, whom he had first met in 1944. Consequently, he refused the earl's petition for divorce.[20] In 1962, Nadine sued for divorce, which was granted in 1963. The earl and Nina were married the same year.

The Premier Earls
Further Notes and Connections

1. For more background on the Dissolution of the Monasteries, see Appendix 7: Dissolution of the Monasteries and The Reformation.

2. In 1383, Richard Talbot, 4th Baron Talbot, married Ankaret Le Strange, the heiress of John Le Strange, 4th Baron Strange of Blackmere. There were 10 children from this marriage, one being John Talbot, who later became the 1st Earl of Shrewsbury. In 1401, Ankaret married Thomas Neville, 6th Baron Furnival. There were two daughters from this marriage - Maud and Joan. Maud married her cousin, the aforementioned John Talbot, thus bringing more wealth to the Talbot family.

3. Goodrich Castle was the chief residence of Sir Richard Talbot, 2nd Baron (d 1356), who was the 1st Earl of Shrewsbury's great grandfather. The Goodrich estates had passed to the Earls of Kent by the 16th century.

4. John, 1st Viscount Lisle, was the son of the 1st Earl of Shrewsbury by his second marriage to Margaret Beauchamp, daughter of the 5th Earl of Warwick, who was a descendant of Edward I. The 1st Earl of Shrewsbury had another son, John, from his first marriage to Maud Nevill. This John became the 2nd Earl of Shrewsbury.

5. The end of the Hundred Years War was followed by the outbreak of the Wars of the Roses, the former being one of the chief causes of the latter.

6. Michael Hicks provides a brief biography of John Talbot, 1st Earl of Shrewsbury, in 'Who's Who In Late Medieval England - 1272-1485': see Acknowledgements below.

7. For more information on the Stafford family and their descendants, see the chapter: "Titles Move In Mysterious Ways".

8. Ingestre came into Shrewsbury family fold via the Chetwynd family, who originated from Chetwynd, near Newport, Shropshire, when Sir Philip de Chetwynd married Isabella de Mutton in the mid 13th century. The Chetwynd and Talbot families came together when John Talbot married Catherine Chetwynd, the heiress daughter of the 2nd Viscount Chetwynd in 1748. There is still much evidence around Ingestre that the Earls of Shrewsbury once lived in the area; the family

name of Chetwynd-Talbot will be immediately recognisable to people living nearby and to people passing through the area from street names and the names of public houses. Some examples of names linked to the family name of the Earls of Shrewsbury: the Chetwynd Arms at Brocton, near Stafford, the Chetwynd Arms at Upper Longdon, the Shrewsbury Arms, Stafford, the Talbot Inn, Cheadle, near Stoke-on-Trent. See also Appendix 2: Public Houses, Roads and Place Names.

9.   The Ingestre estate was extended in 1845 to around 12,000 acres when Earl Talbot purchased the adjoining Tixall estate from Thomas Clifford - see also the chapter: "What's In A Family Name".

10.   Alton became a Shrewsbury possession through the Talbot branch of the family in 1460, when John Talbot, later to become the 1st Earl of Shrewsbury, married his cousin, the heiress, Maud (de) Nevill, through whom he also obtained the title Baron Furnival. Maud's great grandfather, Thomas Furnival, Lord of Sheffield, married the heiress, Joan de Verdun, in 1318. The original Alton Castle had been built by Joan's ancestor, Bertram de Verdun, also spelt as Verdon and Verdum, around 1170. The de Verduns had come over to England with William the Conqueror. The Alton Towers estate was sold in 1924 thus severing a Talbot link of over 500 years and a family link through various female lines to the de Verduns of almost another 300 years.

11.   Other properties, which came into the Talbots' possession, were Salwarp and Grafton in Worcestershire. Talbots from these two branches of the family, who descended from Sir Gilbert Talbot, a younger son of the 2nd Earl of Shrewsbury, provided, respectively, the 9th to 17th Earls of Shrewsbury and the 18th to present day Earls. Salwarp came into the Talbot family via Margaret Beauchamp, the second wife of the 1st Earl of Shrewsbury; Grafton had passed to Gilbert Talbot in 1486 when the Stafford family's estates were forfeited. Humphrey Stafford of Grafton had been executed by order of Henry VII for siding with Richard III. These Staffords were kinsmen of the Dukes of Buckingham - see the chapter: "Titles Move In Mysterious Ways".

12.   Elizabeth Hardwick, Countess of Shrewsbury, c1525-1608, is more commonly referred to as Bess of Hardwick. She was married four times, the most well-known unions being her second and fourth marriages to Sir William Cavendish and the 6th Earl of Shrewsbury, respectively. Bess had six children by Sir William and from these children sprang the dukedoms of Devonshire, Newcastle, Portland and Kingston. She used her very large widow's jointure out of the 6th Earl's will to help

build Hardwick Hall, now in the hands of The National Trust.

13. The counties in which the 6th Earl of Shrewsbury had property included Staffordshire, Shropshire, Worcestershire, Herefordshire, Derbyshire, Nottinghamshire and Yorkshire.

14. The Lambeth Palace Library holds the papers of the Earls of Shrewsbury from the 15th century to the death of Gilbert Talbot, 7th Earl, in 1616. The collection contains hundreds of letters relating to enforced residence of Mary, Queen of Scots, including details of her household, the costs of maintenance (frequently in arrears), the danger of her escape, plans for surveillance, and relations with Elizabeth. During her custody, Mary was moved between the 6th Earl's many houses: Tutbury Castle, Staffordshire, Sheffield Castle, Sheffield Manor, Wingfield Manor, Worksop Manor as well as Chatsworth, the house of his wife, Bess of Hardwick, from her marriage to Sir William Cavendish. After the marriage of the 6th Earl and Bess broke down completely in 1584, the 6th Earl tried to add to his collection of grand houses by making a claim under the terms of their marriage settlement for Chatsworth. However, he failed in this claim.

15. For more information on William Howard, Viscount Stafford, see the chapter: "Titles Move In Mysterious Ways".

16. The 9th Earl of Shrewsbury's sister, Gertrude, married Robert Wintour, one of the Gunpowder Plot conspirators.

17. The 'Immortal Seven' were seven notable English citizens who signed the 'Invitation to William', a document asking William of Orange to depose James II in favour of William's wife Mary, culminating in the Glorious Revolution. The seven were: Thomas Osborne (Earl of Danby), Charles Talbot (12th Earl of Shrewsbury), William Cavendish (Duke of Devonshire); Richard Lumley (Viscount Lumley); Henry Compton (Bishop of London); Edward Russell (Earl of Oxford) and Henry Sidney (Earl of Romney), who wrote the Invitation.

18. For an English county, which is about as far as one can get away from the sea, Staffordshire has probably produced more than its fair share of illustrious sailors. Besides the 18th Earl of Shrewsbury, other Staffordshire families with navy associations include: the Ansons - Admiral George Anson (see also the chapter: "Unfortunate Timing"); the Jervis's - Earl St Vincent; the Leveson-Gowers (see the chapter: "A Family Of Influence") and the Legges.

19. K.P. - Knight of The Most Illustrious Order of St Patrick. The Order was founded in 1783 to reward those in high office in Ireland and

Irish peers on whose support the government of the day depended. It therefore served as the national Order of Ireland as the Garter was for England and the Thistle for Scotland. The Order lapsed in 1974 with the death of the last surviving recipient, Prince Henry, Duke of Gloucester.

20.   In 1960, the 21st Earl of Shrewsbury severed seven hundred years of family association with Ingestre when he sold the estate following the divorce case outlined in the main text of this chapter. This was despite the Countess and her children still living there. The hall is now owned by the Sandwell Metropolitan Council. After the sale, the earl and Nina Mortlock went to live in Madeira, later moving to Switzerland. The 22nd Earl still lives in Staffordshire and, in 2005, the family relationship with Ingestre was renewed when his daughter, Lady Victoria Chetwynd Talbot, was married at the church of St Mary the Virgin, Ingestre, by special licence from the Archbishop of Canterbury, which is usually only granted when there is a family connection with the church. It is believed to be the only church outside London built to a design attributed to Sir Christopher Wren, who was a friend of Walter Chetwynd, who had the church built. Both men were also members of the Royal Society.

The Premier Earls
Acknowledgements

Andrews, Anne (1995), *A History of Tixall - 1. Tixall's Churches,* Hanyards Press; ISBN 0952742519

Chetwynd Stapylton, Henry Edward (1892), *The Chetwynds of Ingestre. Being a History of that Family from a very early date,* Longmans & Co

Gardiner, Juliet - ed (2000), *The History Today Who's Who in British History,* Collins & Brown/CiCo Books; ISBN 1855858827

Girouard, Mark (2004), *Hardwick Hall,* National Trust; ISBN 1843590433

Hicks, Michael A (2001), *Who's Who In Late Medieval England 1272-1485,* Stackpole Books; ISBN 0811716384

Ruscoe, Anthony (2000), *Landed Estates and The Gentry - An Historical Study of the Landed Estates of North East Shropshire: Volume 4;* ISBN 0953050246

Salter, Mike (1997), T*he Castles and Moated Mansions of Staffordshire,* Folly Publications; ISBN 1871731291

Wrenn, Dorothy P H (1975), *Shropshire History Makers,* EP Publishing Ltd; ISBN 0715810960

Daily Telegraph Obituaries; 2003

Rotherham website http://www.rotherhamweb.co.uk/h/index.htm (accessed 2004)

Church of England - Lambeth Palace Library website

http://www.lambethpalacelibrary.org/ (accessed 2004/05)

Further Reading

Fisher, Michael (1999), *Alton Towers – A Gothic Wonderland,* M J Fisher; ISBN 0952685523

Michael Fisher (2004), *Perfect Cheadle – St Giles' Catholic Church, Cheadle, Staffordshire,* M J Fisher, ISBN 095268554X

Fisher, Michael (2002), *Pugin-Land,* M J Fisher; ISBN 0952685531

Haggar, Mark S, *The fortunes of a Norman family: the de Verduns in England, Ireland and Wales, 1066-1316,* Four Courts Press; ISBN 1851825967

TALBOT/CHETWYND-TALBOT FAMILIES

SUMMARY FAMILY TREE SHOWING RELATIONSHIP BETWEEN THE 17TH AND 18TH EARLS OF SHREWSBURY AND THEIR FOREBEARS

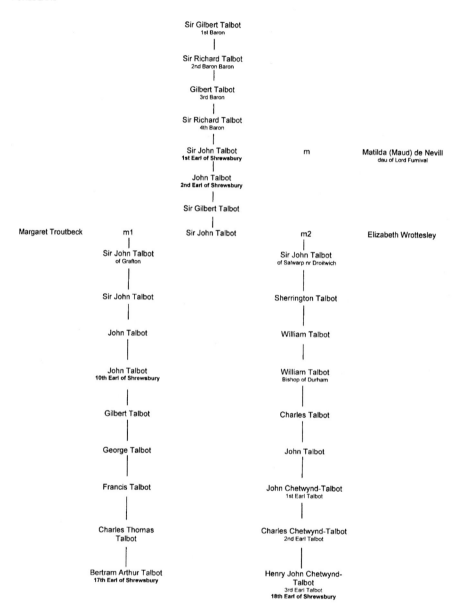

Sir Gilbert Talbot
1st Baron

Sir Richard Talbot
2nd Baron Baron

Gilbert Talbot
3rd Baron

Sir Richard Talbot
4th Baron

Sir John Talbot   m   Matilda (Maud) de Nevill
1st Earl of Shrewsbury   dau of Lord Furnival

John Talbot
2nd Earl of Shrewsbury

Sir Gilbert Talbot

Margaret Troutbeck   m1   Sir John Talbot   m2   Elizabeth Wrottesley

Sir John Talbot   Sir John Talbot
of Grafton   of Salwarp nr Droitwich

Sir John Talbot   Sherrington Talbot

John Talbot   William Talbot

John Talbot   William Talbot
10th Earl of Shrewsbury   Bishop of Durham

Gilbert Talbot   Charles Talbot

George Talbot   John Talbot

Francis Talbot   John Chetwynd-Talbot
                                       1st Earl Talbot

Charles Thomas   Charles Chetwynd-Talbot
Talbot   2nd Earl Talbot

Bertram Arthur Talbot   Henry John Chetwynd-
17th Earl of Shrewsbury   Talbot
                                       3rd Earl Talbot
                                       18th Earl of Shrewsbury

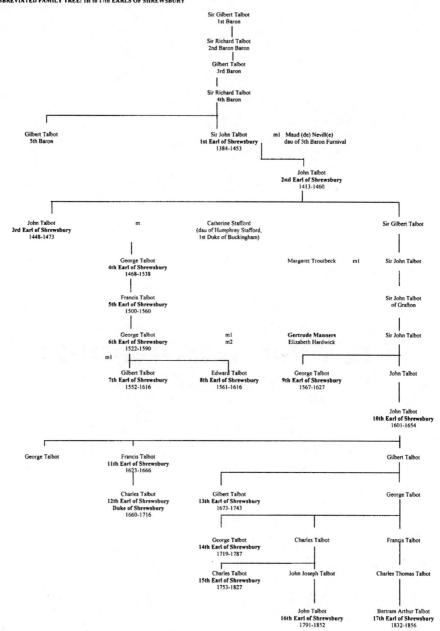

PART 2

A FEW NON-STAFFORDSHIRE FAMILIES

What's In A Title, Anyway?

The future of the Earldom of Selkirk, with its seat in the House of Lords, a £500,000 inheritance and family heirlooms, was decided after the Lord Lyon studied two 17th century Latin documents.[1]

On 4 January 1996, the Court of Lord Lyon, the Scottish College of Heralds, sat in a rare public hearing to hear the arguments of the then current Master of Selkirk, Alasdair Douglas-Hamilton, and his first cousin, the then MP Lord James Douglas-Hamilton.

Lord James claimed that since the 10th Earl, his uncle, died in 1994 without a son, the title should go through his line as younger brother of the present Duke of Hamilton. Alisdair Douglas-Hamilton is the son of Malcolm, the 10th Earl's younger brother. He had been named as heir by both Burke's and Debrett's Peerage.

The matter was complicated because Lord James had said he would renounce the title since taking it would mean resigning his seat in the Commons posing a further threat to the then Conservative Government's slim majority. He wanted the title for his 17 years old son, John Andrew.

Addressing the Lord Lyon King of Arms, Sir Malcolm Innes of Edingight, in Edinburgh, barristers for the cousins agreed that rules of succession drawn up in Latin in the 17th century for Charles I in 1646 and then for James II in 1688 were crucial to the case.

William Douglas, a staunch Royalist, was created Earl of Selkirk by Charles I, with a diploma bearing the rules of succession. But when William later married Anne, Duchess of Hamilton in her own right, she successfully petitioned for him to be created the Duke of Hamilton, at which time he also received several of the other Hamilton peerages, but for his lifetime only; the earldom of Selkirk also became a subsidiary title. James, their son, became the 4th Duke of Hamilton after his mother resigned the dukedom to him in 1698, four years after his father had died.

In 1688, James II of England and VII of Scotland re-granted the earldom to reward the Douglas-Hamilton family for its loyalty. The diploma in this case contained a proviso that the inheritance should go to the younger brothers of the duke so that the two titles, wherever possible, would be held separately. The document named the Duke's heirs for the earldom as his younger brothers 'et heredes masculos ex eius corpore' (and male heirs of his body). From 1688 until the 10th Earl's death in November 1994, the earldom moved down the line of brothers without any problems.

But when the 10th Earl died, it became apparent that, with no children himself, the succession would not be so simple.

Professor John Murray, QC, for Alisdair Douglas-Hamilton, said his client was the rightful heir because his father would have succeeded had he lived. The Latin proviso meant that the title should go through brothers other than the duke wherever possible.

He also argued that, although the diploma named specific heirs, this should not have an immediate bearing on the succession hundreds of years later; the aim of the document to keep the two titles separate was the most important factor.

Mr Murray told the Lord Lyon that both Burke's Peerage and Debretts had named Alisdair Douglas-Hamilton as heir and that he had used the title Master of Selkirk since the death of his father, Malcolm, the third son of Alfred, the 13th Duke of Hamilton and, for a period, the 9th Earl of Selkirk.

William Nimmo Smith, QC, for Lord James, said a tighter interpretation of the words 'male heir of the body' was required.

As the 10th Earl left no immediate male heirs, the correct procedure was to go back to the creation of the earldom in 1646 and find the male heir from that line of the family, he said.

By following these rules, the current heir would be Angus, the 15th and current Duke and brother of Lord James. But as it was deemed that he should not hold both titles, it should go to his younger brother, Lord James, and then his son.

"The proviso provides for the immediate younger brother and his heirs, male, of the body, to succeed" said. Mr Nimmo Smith. "Its destination is not to the heir males or whoever but quite specific."'

"So each time the succession opens, the destination goes back to the institution of the earldom and you go back through the family tree to find the current male heir."

On Thursday, 14 March 1996, the Court of Lord Lyon delivered its judgement in favour of Lord James Douglas-Hamilton.

Despite the wrangling over the title and the 10th Earl's legacy, both men claimed that they had remained on good terms.

During the action, Lord James had said: "As a former advocate, I am concerned that the correct decision is made."

As noted earlier, the outcome made no difference to Lord James personally - his decision to disclaim the title rather than force a by-election in his constituency could not be reversed. Nor can his son inherit the title until Lord James dies. The decision not to force a by-election became academic the following year, as Lord James lost his seat in the Labour landslide general election of 1997. Lord James Douglas-Hamilton was subsequently created a life peer: Lord Selkirk of Douglas.[2]

Mr Douglas-Hamilton said he had not been motivated by the money involved, said to be £500,000.

What's In A Title, Anyway?
Further Notes and Connections

1. See Appendix 1: Hereditary Titles for more information on inheritance of titles. The abbreviated family tree, which follows this chapter, shows the relationships of the Dukes of Hamilton and Earls of Selkirk. The two 'protagonists' in the court case are highlighted in bold print.
2. The wife of Lord Selkirk of Douglas, who would have been the 11th Earl of Selkirk but for his disclaimer, is the granddaughter of John Buchan, 1st Lord Tweedsmuir, the author of the Richard Hannay stories, the best known being 'The Thirty Nine Steps'.

What's In A Title, Anyway?
Acknowledgements

Daily Telegraph
Mail on Sunday

THE DUKES OF HAMILTON AND EARLS OF SELKIRK

ABBREVIATED FAMILY TREE

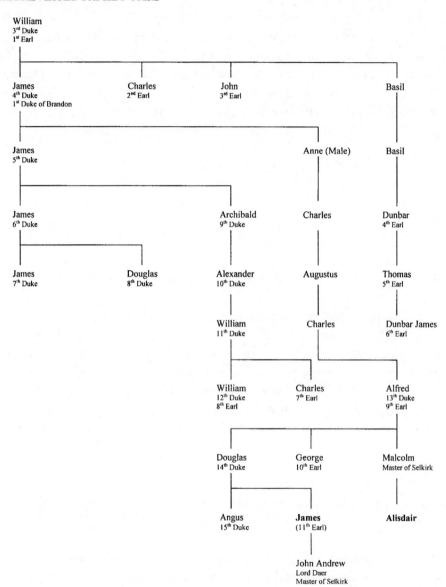

The Lord Who Nearly Prevented World War 2

The 9th Lord Howard de Walden and 5th Lord Seaford died in 1999 at the age of 86. He was a prominent racehorse owner, a former Senior Steward of the Jockey Club and one of Britain's richest landlords, owning more than 100 acres of Marylebone in central London. This estate runs between Oxford Street and the Marylebone Road, encompassing Cavendish Square, as well as the medical districts of Harley Street, Wimpole Street and the Middlesex Hospital.

A couple of anecdotes about the 9th Lord follow.

In 1931, when he was studying as a language student in Munich, he hit a pedestrian whilst out driving with a German friend: the man got up and walked off. His German companion said: "I do not suppose you know who that was? He is a politician with a party and he talks a lot. His name is Adolf Hitler." What might have happened if Hitler's injuries had been fatal?

Before going to Magdalene College, Cambridge, he was despatched to visit the extensive farming interests his father, the 8th Lord, had acquired in Kenya. There he encountered the denizens of Happy Valley, whose louche behaviour he put down to the altitude.[1] Arriving to stay with new acquaintances, he was greeted by the butler with "Good evening, sir. And who will you be sleeping with tonight?" He later wrote that he had spent the years since wondering what a good reply would have been; perhaps, "Please show me the menu."

The 8th Baron, who fought in the Boer War and at Gallipoli, was a man of exceptional range - a mediaevalist, champion fencer, power-boat racer, explorer, painter and author of opera libretti on Byzantine themes, as well as a shrewd investor, man of the Turf and steward of the Jockey Club.

Despite his immense wealth, the 8th Lord Howard de Walden lacked a country seat of his own, so he rented Chirk Castle. It was there that John, the future 9th Baron, and his five sisters were brought up. The guests at Chirk during John's childhood included Augustus John, the painter. Descending to breakfast one morning the painter was surprised to find Lord Howard de Walden reading the newspaper while wearing a full suit of armour - yet another of his enthusiasms.

The 9th Lord's mother, Margherita, was as colourful as her husband and as distant to her children. She was a talented singer and, in later life, she was in the habit of performing cartwheels on the battlements at Chirk Castle.

Elizabeth I created the barony of Howard de Walden in 1597 for Admiral Thomas Howard, a younger son of the 4th Duke of Norfolk. The title was reportedly granted for the Admiral's role in the defeat of the Spanish Armada. In 1603, Thomas was created Earl of Suffolk by James I of England. As Lord Chamberlain, the Earl of Suffolk, led the search, which led to the arrest of Guy Fawkes and the eventual collapse of the Gunpowder Plot. [2,3]

The barony was one of the last to be created by Writ of Summons, as a result of which, in the absence of a son, the peerage follows common law in devolving on a daughter, rather than on collateral male heirs. Where there is no son but more than one daughter (as in the 9th Lord's case), the peerage goes into abeyance. The title has passed through the female line several times.

Following the death of the 3rd Earl of Suffolk without surviving sons or heirs male of his body, the earldom passed to his brother. However, the barony of Howard de Walden fell into abeyance from 1689 until 1734, when it was called out of abeyance for a descendant of the third Earl's elder daughter, Lady Essex Howard, later Baroness Griffin, having passed through the female line to the Earls of Bristol. Thereafter, it passed to the Ellis family when a granddaughter of the 4th Earl of Bristol married Charles Ellis, an MP and later the 1st Lord Seaford, in 1798. The son of that marriage succeeded as the 6th Lord Howard de Walden. In 1828, he married Lady Lucy Cavendish-Bentinck, daughter of the 4th Duke of Portland, whose dowry included the Marylebone estate.[3] By Royal Warrant dated 25 June 25 2004, Her Majesty The Queen called the barony of Howard de Walden out of abeyance in favour of the eldest daughter, Mary Hazel Caridwen Czernin (born 1935).

The Lord Who Nearly Prevented World War 2
Further Notes and Connections

1. See also the chapter: "The Happy Valley Connection" for a Staffordshire link with the behaviour of the rich white settlers in the so-called Happy Valley region of Kenya.
2. Later Howard Earls of Suffolk obtained Staffordshire interests through the marriage of Craven Howard to Mary Bowes, heiress of the Elford estate near Tamworth. Their son, Henry Bowes Howard, became the 11th Earl of Suffolk. See also the chapter: "Titles Move In Mysterious Ways" for another Staffordshire branch of the Howard family.
3. The Gunpowder Plot also had a Staffordshire connection in Holbeche House at Wall Heath, near Kingswinford, the site of the last stand for some of the conspirators, including the leader, Robert (Robin) Catesby, Thomas Percy and the Wright brothers. This was the home of Stephen Littleton. The house is now a private nursing home.
4. The Dukes of Portland's family name was Cavendish-Bentinck; they were kinsmen of the Cavendishes, who were eventually created Dukes of Devonshire. The Portland Dukedom has now become extinct.

The Lord Who Nearly Prevented World War 2
Acknowledgements

Fraser, Antonia (2004), *The Gunpowder Plot,* Phoenix; ISBN 0753814013

Daily Telegraph

The Original James Bond?

Sir Fitzroy Maclean, 1st Baronet and 15th Captain and Hereditary Keeper of Dunconnel in the Isles of the Sea, who died aged 85 in 1996, led an extraordinarily glamorous career as diplomat, soldier, politician and traveller.

The young Fitzroy Maclean was born in Egypt and brought up in Scotland, India and Italy. From his mother he gained a love and facility for languages. All these experiences and attributes helped to engender a life of adventure.

He was educated at Eton and King's College, Cambridge. Afterwards, in 1933, he joined the Foreign Office during which he was posted to the British embassy in Paris. Bored with the pleasant but undemanding routine, he requested a posting to Moscow, which would later become the basis for the autobiographical 'Eastern Approaches', [1] his best-known book. It was during his time in Russia that he learnt to speak Russian fluently. MacLean was in Moscow until late 1939, and was present during the great Stalinist purges, observing the fates of Nikolai Bukharin, who was executed in 1938, and other Russian revolutionaries. During his posting to Moscow, MacLean ventured by train and by foot into often-remote regions of the Soviet Union, which were off limits to foreigners, and was pursued by the NKVD as he did so.

On the outbreak of the Second World War, he was not allowed to join the army because his post in the Diplomatic Service was a reserved occupation. However, in 1941, he discovered that, if he declared his wish to stand as a parliamentary candidate, he would be obliged to resign from the Foreign Office. Having stated this intention in his letter of resignation, Maclean enlisted as a private in the Cameron Highlanders. Remembering these early army days, Maclean observed: "At meal times, we threw ourselves on our food like a pack of wolves and, wherever we were given a chance, we slept: indoors, out of doors, in broad daylight, in the middle of a room full of men shouting, singing and swearing". But Maclean was unconcerned: "At Eton, you know, there is a tougher ambience".

After several months, he was given a commission, only to discover that the Foreign Office had called his bluff and were now trying to get him back from the Army. Maclean was now forced to renew his efforts to get into Parliament.

Fortune was on his side as there was a by-election pending at Lancaster. He won the Conservative nomination and, much to his astonishment, was elected.

However, before he was able to take his seat, he was sent on a mission to Cairo, where he bumped into Colonel David Sterling, [2] who had just formed the SAS (Special Air Service) for raiding enemy installations deep in the Western Desert. Maclean joined, and was soon engaged in hazardous operations. On one occasion, he and a few others made their way with a truckload of explosives to Benghazi, which was in enemy hands, with the intention of blowing up installations in the harbour. When an Italian sentry challenged them, Maclean informed him they were staff officers and demanded to see the guard commander. When the latter appeared, Maclean upbraided him in fluent Italian for dereliction of duty, saying that they had been walking around all night in the area for which the guard was responsible without once being challenged or asked to produce identity cards. Maclean then added, "For all you know, we might have been British saboteurs carrying explosives." When the guard commander tittered incredulously, Maclean said he would let him off this time but he had better not be caught napping again.

At the end of the desert campaign, Maclean was sent to Persia, now Iran, where he frustrated a coup by the pro-German General Zahidi.

Soon afterwards, in July 1943, Winston Churchill chose Maclean for a secret mission to Tito, leader of the Partisans in Yugoslavia. Churchill had a single clear aim. Maclean summed up Churchill's instructions as follows: "My task was simply to find out who was killing the most Germans and suggest means by which we could help them to kill more." However, despite Churchill's clear objectives, this did not prevent the Foreign Office from being at odds with the Special Operations Executive (SOE). Long after the war, Maclean discovered that the SOE referred to the Foreign Office as the enemy.

On the ground in occupied Yugoslavia, Maclean became a firm friend of Tito, whom he regarded as probably the greatest guerrilla/resistance fighter of all time. He believed that part of Tito's greatness was imposing order out of the complexity of events in the 1940s and the ensuing bloodshed and chaos. During this time, Maclean, too, had to impose himself on the disparate elements under his command. His officer in charge of supplies remembered: "Fitzroy was immensely physically fit. He had immense confidence, was charismatic, and knew the Establishment inside out. Extraordinarily nice man. Although he was firm and clear in his aims, he never raised his voice. When he asked you to do something, it was quite clear that he meant now."

Even so, there were those who resented Maclean's speedy elevation to brigadier. Maclean gave himself more trouble by recruiting Randolph Churchill, the Prime Minister's son, for his mission to Yugoslavia. Not only was the younger Churchill extraordinarily difficult and quarrelsome on his own account, he in his turn recruited Evelyn Waugh. As W F Deedes states in his book: 'At War with Waugh: The Real Story of Scoop' Waugh was never popular with his brother officers, nor was his Army career distinguished, but no one ever doubted his physical courage.

Waugh, by this time a committed Roman Catholic convert with a horror of Bolshevism, took an instant dislike to his commander. In his diary, he wrote: "Maclean dour, unprincipled, ambitious, probably very wicked; shaved head and devil's ears." Waugh also propagated the notion that Tito was a woman. But Maclean was able to score heavily on this issue for when Waugh was introduced to the Partisan leader, he was for once left speechless by Tito's question: "And why do you think I am a woman?" Maclean had proved that he was tough and ruthless enough to handle even the most brilliant dissident. Even so, Maclean later helped to save Waugh from a court-martial.

From all of his exploits, it is not difficult to see why many people believe that Fitzroy Maclean was the inspiration for Ian Fleming's legendary secret agent, James Bond. In a BBC Radio Scotland interview, his widow stated that while 'Fitz' revelled in the idea that he had provided the template for 007, he had never been a spy himself. He used to love that rumour. He enjoyed it very much. We always had a travelling vodka set wherever we went, and that was very Bond-like. Lady Veronica also revealed that Sir Fitzroy, like Bond, had 'an eye for the ladies and was very, very brave' but was scarred by his experiences behind enemy lines during the war: "If there was a noise in the night that woke him, he'd roll out of bed with his hands in a defensive position."

It is also said that his exploits provided the basis for Alistair MacLean's best selling novel, "The Guns of Navarone".

The Original James Bond?
Further Notes and Connections

1. 'Eastern Approaches' is an account of Fitzroy Maclean's time as a young diplomat in Russia before World War II including his travels through Eastern Russia and Siberia. It includes his encounters with the people and his historical descriptions as well as material on his transfer to Cairo and the war in the Western desert. Finally, it deals with his time in Yugoslavia.

2. David Sterling's daring exploits with the SAS have been captured in Virginia Cowles's book 'The Phantom Major', first published in 1958. Fitzroy Maclean is mentioned on numerous occasions.

The Original James Bond?
Acknowledgements

Daily Telegraph

BBC Radio Scotland

Further Reading

Cowles, Virginia (1989), *The Phantom Major,* Armada; ISBN 0006935192

Maclean, Fitzroy (2004), *Eastern Approaches,* Penguin Books; ISBN 0140132716

The Human Cannonball

The Cistercian Order of Monks came to Wales towards the middle of the twelfth century and, by 1170, had established eight abbeys in the southern half of the country. They were popular amongst the Barons and minor Princes who ruled over Wales and who were only too ready to grant to the Order tracts of land on which they could establish new foundations. Llywelyn ab Iorwerth (Llewelyn the Great) is said to have founded the abbey at Conwy, where he was buried in 1240. It is also recorded that, in 1284, Edward I removed the monks from Aberconwy to Maenan, where they completed the largest and what is claimed to be the most beautiful of Welsh monasteries.

In a charter, dated 1198, Llywelyn gave some 1,000 acres of land in the area of the monastic buildings, as well as numerous granges scattered around Gwynedd. To the east of Conwy, the Creuddyn grange provided some 1,200 acres, whilst the Dolgarrog grange provided them with 3,800 acres. Four further granges added another 17,000 acres.

Llywelyn also gave other grants and rights to the order. The Abbey of Aberconwy was granted churches, mills, fishing rights, freedom from tools, freedom from having to provide the Prince and his court with food, freedom from secular interference in internal matters, rights of shipwreck plus many other rights.

Llywelyn's charter to Aberconwy was extremely generous. It is believed that it was his intention to create an exceptionally powerful establishment and it soon became the most important monastery in North Wales as well as the burial place of the Princes of Gwynedd.

The 14th and 15th centuries brought financial difficulties for the Abbey. By March 1537, the Abbey had been dissolved during Henry VIII's Dissolution of the Monasteries.[1] The land was sold off by the Crown and the monastic buildings were demolished, the timber and stone being taken to repair Caernarfon Castle.

The site of the Abbey and the adjacent land passed to the Wynnes of Melai.

In 1736, the heiress of the Wynne family married Sir John Wynn of Bodfaen in west Caernarfonshire; their son was created Lord Newborough and the Newboroughs owned Maenan Abbey until the early years of the twentieth century.

The 1st Lord Newborough built up interests in the slate industry, which were carried on by his sons, the 2nd and 3rd Lords Newborough.

As Sub-Lieutenant Mickey Wynn, the later 7th Lord Newborough, fought in World War II. He was awarded the DSC (Distinguished Service Cross) for his part in the daring and brilliantly successful cross-channel raid on the huge dry-dock at St Nazaire, France, which was carried out by British Commando and Naval Forces in March 1942. This action, code-named Operation Chariot, lifted Britain's morale and demonstrated that bravery could achieve the apparently impossible. Five Victoria Crosses were won on the raid, the largest number ever awarded for a single action. In fact, the operation was so successful that the dock could not be used again before war's end. The importance to Britain's war effort was that St Nazaire was one of only a handful of ports throughout the world, which possessed dry docks large enough to house the battleship Tirpitz should she, like her sister-ship 'Bismarck' ever be damaged in battle: and, of these, the only one, which could be accessed directly from the Atlantic. By destroying the massive dry dock built there to house the liner 'Normandie', the 'Tirpitz' would be forced to return all the way to Germany for repair. This would require her to run the gauntlet of air and sea patrols, and of the waiting Home Fleet, and it was judged that her masters might well rethink their plans to sail her. Of the 611 soldiers and sailors who took part in Operation Chariot, 169 were killed and 200, most of whom were wounded, were taken prisoner. Only 242 returned immediately to British shores. Sub-Lieutenant Wynn was one of those captured. He was later transferred to Colditz Castle in January 1943, where he was imprisoned until he was repatriated in January 1945.

In 1998, a report was published on the Princeton University website about what was claimed to be one of the world's greatest unrecognised sporting events: Delaware's annual Punkin' Chunkin' contest, in which participants build cannons of various sorts and then fire pumpkins from them. The winning cannon that year was the Aludium Q36 Pumpkin Modulator, which set a record with a pumpkin launch of 4,026 feet, according to USA Today. The report went on to comment that even the best American zaniness could not hope to compete with British eccentricity, as the late (7th) Lord Newborough had proven

145

posthumously. Lord Newborough had specified that his ashes be inserted into a steel canister and shot from a cannon into the woods on his estate; his son, the new Lord Newborough, complied, but the eighteenth-century ordnance he used burst into flames upon firing. The report concluded that, perhaps the next time this sort of burial took place, the bereaved should invest in an Aludium Q36 Corpse Modulator.

On the 7th Baron's death, the new Lord Newborough inherited the Rhug Estate at Corwen, Denbighshire. The 8th Lord Newborough was very quick to see the future for the estate and oversaw every detail of the organic conversion of the farm.

The Human Cannonball
Further Notes and Connections

1. For further information on the Dissolution of the Monasteries and the Reformation, see the Appendix of the same name.
2. Bardsey Island (Ynys Enlli in Welsh), off the tip of the Lleyn Peninsula across Bardsey Sound, was once owned by Lord Newborough. It was sold to the Bardsey Island Trust. It is now a place of outstanding natural beauty, of rare sea birds, of precious flora and fauna, of seals and dolphins.

The Human Cannonball
Acknowledgements

Princeton University website (accessed 2004)

The St Nazaire Society website http://www.stnazairesociety.org/ (accessed 2004)

James G Dorrian website http://www.jamesdorrian.co.uk/ (accessed 2004)

Who Died First?

The 3rd Lord Stamp, Emeritus Professor of Bacteriology at London University, who died in 1987 at the age of 80, was a distinguished medical scientist, a public-spirited peer and sometime president of the Liberal party, as well as a dedicated teacher, an assiduous administrator and fundraiser known as 'the Stamp Collector".

He was best known for his research into vaccinations against infections with staphylococci and streptococci, and, though not a clinician, had a long-held interest in tropical diseases. During the Second World War, Stamp was engaged in important secret research work at Porton Down.

In a debate on chemical and biological warfare in the House of Lords in 1969, Lord Stamp said that he had become involved in this work in 1941 when there were grounds for believing that this weapon might be used against us by a ruthless enemy. "A failure to take measures for protection then would have been criminal negligence", he said.

It was in the same year, 1941, that Stamp unexpectedly succeeded to the peerage created for his father, Sir Josiah Stamp, the economist, when both his parents, his elder brother and four members of their domestic staff were killed in a direct hit on their home in Bromley during an air raid. Consequently, the precise order of the succession of the peerage had to be decided by the House of Lords.

Their Lordships ruled that the 1st Lord Stamp's eldest son, Wilfrid, had 'succeeded momentarily' to the title and that therefore his widow and daughters would enjoy the appropriate status, styles and titles derived from their relationship with the 2nd Baron. This also meant that the family had to pay two lots of death duties The second son, Trevor, was duly called to the peerage as the 3rd Lord Stamp.

Born in 1907, Trevor Charles Stamp was educated at the Leys School, Cambridge, and Gonville and Caius College, Cambridge, before qualifying as a doctor at St Bartholomew's Hospital. He soon decided to specialise in bacteriology and joined the staff of the London School of Hygiene and Tropical

Medicine as a demonstrator in bacteriology in 1932, and became a lecturer in 1934.

Besides his teaching commitments he was also engaged in research and made some original observations on sulphonamides, which were at that time, before the development of antibiotics, the only effective treatment against bacterial infection.

Stamp adopted a remarkably modem approach to examining the role of chemical fractions of the bacteria and of local factors, such as oxidation-reduction potential in the tissues. One of his early works was a simple method of storing bacteria dried in gelatine pellets: suitable strains would still be alive twenty or more years later.

After the war, Lord Stamp resumed his post as Reader in Bacteriology and he was appointed Professor of Bacteriology, London University, and Chairman of the Pathology Department at the Royal Post Graduate Medical School in 1948, continued to occupy the Chair of Bacteriology until his retirement in 1970.

He particularly enjoyed the international flavour of teaching young doctors from all over the Commonwealth, remaining in contact with them and following their careers in their own countries with great interest, giving them advice and encouragement.

He also travelled widely both as a scientist and as a member of the Parliamentary delegation of the Inter-Parliamentary Union, with whom he toured Egypt, Tokyo, Sofia, Prague and Caracas.

Lord Stamp was an active member of the House of Lords, taking a particular interest in African affairs and health matters. In 1954, he introduced the Protection of Animals (Anaesthetics Bill), which stipulated that, with minor exceptions, animal operations must be performed under anaesthesia.

Originally a Liberal (he was elected president of the party in 1957), he later became a crossbencher though his utterances in the chamber tended to reflect views more akin to the right wing of the Conservatives. Thus he opposed the abolition of the death penalty, sanctions against Rhodesia, the miners' strike and the free issue of contraceptives to students.

Lord Stamp had a deep concern for education and was for many years a governor of the girls' school, Queenswood, Herts, to which he devoted much time and energy. A modestly kindly figure, he lived up to his name by being a keen philatelist, but gave up the hobby when his collection was stolen in the 1950s.

He married in 1932, Frances Dawes Bosworth, from Evanston, Illinois, who survived him together with their two sons. Their elder son, Dr Trevor Charles Bosworth Stamp, succeeded to the peerage as the 4th Baron Stamp.

Who Died First?
Acknowledgements

Daily Telegraph

APPENDICES

Appendix 1:   Hereditary Titles

Appendix 2:   Public Houses and Roads

Appendix 3:   The Demise of the English Country House

Appendix 4:   The Cliffords

Appendix 5:   The Blounts

Appendix 6:   Great Offices of State of England

Appendix 7:   Dissolution of the Monasteries & The Reformation

Appendix 8:   Glossary of Terms

Appendix 9:   Kings, Queens and Rulers of England and Great Britain

Appendix 10:   The Industrial Revolution and the Development of the Country's Transport Infrastructure

Appendix 11:   Some Introductory Notes to other Staffordshire Families

Appendix 1
Hereditary Titles
Introduction

Hereditary titles are those, which pass from one generation to the next, usually in direct succession through the male line.

The rules, which govern the creation and succession of peerages, are extremely complicated. However, in general terms, the mode of inheritance of a hereditary peerage is determined by the method of its creation. Titles may be created by Writ of Summons or by Letters Patent.

A Writ of Summons is merely a summons of an individual to Parliament - it does not explicitly confer a peerage-and descent is always to *heirs of the body*, male and female. Normally, in the absence of a son, the peerage follows common law in devolving on a daughter, rather than on collateral male heirs. Where there is no son but more than one daughter, the peerage goes into abeyance.[1,2]

The Letters Patent method is used to explicitly create a peerage and name the dignity in question. Letters Patent may state the course of descent; normally, only male heirs are allowed to succeed to the peerage. In all cases, only legitimate children may succeed to a title. Under Scottish law, an illegitimate child is legitimated by a future marriage of the parents. Under English and British law, however, a child is illegitimate if the parents are unmarried at the time of birth, and remains illegitimate even after a marriage between them. Thus, an illegitimate child may succeed to a Scottish peerage, but not an English, Irish or British one, if the parents marry after the birth.

Every title is granted with a 'remainder', which gives the instructions as to whom the title passes when the original holder dies. Remainders can be rather general, such as 'To heirs whatsoever', which would allow the title to pass to either male or female descendants, or very specific, such as 'To heirs male of the first son, failing that, to heirs male of the third son'. A remainder like this was given to the Duchess of Cleveland by Charles II because there was some doubt as to the father of her second child.

However, as a generalisation, the following summarises the order in which titles often pass on the death of the titleholder:

1. Eldest son

2. Eldest son's eldest son

3. Eldest son's eldest son's eldest son (etc.)

4. Second son

5. Second son's eldest son

6. Second son's eldest son's eldest son (etc.)

7. Remaining sons in order (etc. etc.)

8. Eldest brother

9. Eldest brother's eldest son (etc. etc.)

10. Second eldest brother (etc. etc. etc.)

11. Eldest surviving male directly descended through the male line from the original titleholder (not the closest male relative)

As stated above, this is a generalisation but it does show how uncles, great-uncles or distant cousins can inherit the title. The heir is sometimes very difficult to determine. The process occasionally results in long and costly fights in Lords with different branches of the family presenting conflicting evidence in support of their claim e.g. the claim to the Earldom of Selkirk - see the chapter: "What's In A Title, Anyway?"

A title becomes *extinct* when all possible heirs (as provided by the letters patent) have died out. A title becomes *dormant* if no person has claimed the title, or if no claim has been satisfactorily proven. A title goes into *abeyance* if there is more than one person equally qualified to be the holder.

The Peerage

The Peerage in the United Kingdom comprises all the Lords or persons raised in class and considered to be 'Peers of the Monarch'.

The Peerage used to be easily defined as those who held a seat in the House of Lords. However, after the House of Lords Act, 1999, the right of most hereditary peers to be a member of the House of Lords was abolished.

In addition to members of the Peerage, the title of Baronet is usually hereditary. However, a baronet could hold a seat in the House of Commons as a Member of Parliament (MP), whereas a Peer could not, although the heir to a peerage could be an MP until he succeeded to the title.

However, the Peerage Act 1963, enabled peers to disclaim their peerages for life. The disclaimer is irrevocable but does not affect the descent of the peerage after the disclaimant's death, and children of a disclaimed peer may, if they wish, retain their precedence and any courtesy titles and styles borne as children of a peer. The disclaimer permits the disclaimant to sit in the House of Commons as an MP. When a peerage has been disclaimed, no other hereditary peerage shall be conferred. Anthony Wedgwood-Benn (Tony Benn), the left-wing Labour MP, whose father, the 1st Lord Stansgate, died in 1960, took advantage of this Act so that he could return to the House of Commons. Quinton Hogg, the 2nd Viscount Hailsham, disclaimed his hereditary peerages in 1963, in order to sit in the House of Commons as a Conservative MP. In 1970, he was appointed Lord Chancellor and received the customary life peerage, becoming Lord Hailsham of St Marylebone. A life peerage cannot be disclaimed.

Order of Precedence

Tables of Precedence have some merit when placing people at official and special occasions. Nonetheless, they contain many traps for the unwary. For example, a Baron ranks below a Viscount. However, if the person is a Baron in his own right, perhaps created for services rendered, but is also a Duke's younger son, the latter precedence is above a Viscount and thus takes priority.

For the Peerage, the order of precedence, in its simplest terms, is:

Dukes

Marquesses

Earls

Viscounts

Barons (or Lord of Parliament in the Peerage of Scotland)

Note: All Life Peers are Barons or Baronesses

Baronets, who are not Peers, follow after Barons/Baronesses.

Forms of Address and Courtesy Titles

This area of social etiquette is a minefield for even the well-read person and I would always recommend referring to a recognised publication such as 'Debrett's Correct Form'. A brief introduction is given below.

Dukes are addressed as 'My Lord Duke' or 'Your Grace'. The eldest sons of Dukes, Marquesses and Earls take, by courtesy, their father's second title. The other sons and daughters of Dukes and Marquesses are styled 'Lord' or 'Lady' before their forename e.g. Lord Edward ...., Lady Caroline ...., whereas the other sons of Earls are styled as 'The Honourable', usually abbreviated to 'The Hon.' e.g. The Hon. John ..... and the daughters Lady Elizabeth ..... et.c.

Peers of the grades of Marquess, Earl, Viscount and Baron are all addressed formally as 'My Lord' and socially as 'Lord ....' e.g. Lord Lichfield, who is the Earl of Lichfield. The use of their exact rank is socially incorrect; it is, however, used on envelopes, visiting cards and invitations. The fifth grade of the peerage, a Baron, is never referred to by this title, except in legal or formal documents but always as Lord e.g. Lord Stafford, who is a Baron by rank. In the Peerage of Scotland, the term 'Lord' (Lord of Parliament) is the legal term for the fifth grade in the peerage, because the term 'Baron' is used in a feudal sense relating to land tenure.

The eldest sons of Viscounts and Barons have no distinctive title; they, as well as their brothers and sisters, are styled as The Hon. Robert ...., The Hon. Mary .... etc.

Hereditary Titles
Further Notes and Connections

1. Where a peerage has fallen into abeyance and one of the co-heirs wishes to have the abeyance terminated in his favour, a formal petition, addressed to the Sovereign, has to be submitted, together with evidence supporting the claim, through the Home Office. The matter is then referred to the Attorney General, the evidence in the case being examined by the Treasury Solicitor. If there are no problems with the petition, the Attorney General may make a direct recommendation that the royal discretion be exercised. If there are any doubts, the claim is submitted to the Committee for Privileges.

2. For an example of what happens following a title going into abeyance, see the chapter: "The Lord Who Nearly Prevented World War 2".

Hereditary Titles
Acknowledgements

Montague-Smith Patrick - ed. (1992), *Debrett's Correct Form,* Headline Book Publishing PLC; ISBN 0747206589

Debrett's Peerage & Baronetage 2000

Whitaker's Almanac

'*Addressing the Duke and Inheriting his Loot,*' *a guide to English titles, forms of address and inheritance laws during the Regency period.* Presented by Emily Hendrickson and Al Lansdowne at the Beau Monde Conference 'A Regency Mill' on 28 July 1999.

Appendix 2
Public Houses, Roads and Place Names

A sample of the various public houses, streets and place names named after, or linked to, Staffordshire aristocrats and landed gentry is given below:

Public Houses and Inns

The Clifford Arms, Great Haywood, near Stafford - Clifford family, kinsmen of the Lords Clifford

The Wolseley Arms, Wolseley Bridge, near Stafford - Wolseley baronets

The Jerningham Arms, Shifnal, near Telford, Shropshire - Lords Stafford

The Fitzherbert Arms, Swynnerton, Staffordshire - Lords Stafford

The Swynnerton Arms, Rough Close - Lords Stafford

The Shrewsbury Arms - numerous places including Stafford - Earls of Shrewsbury

The Chetwynd Arms, Brocton, near Stafford - Earls of Shrewsbury

The Chetwynd Arms, Upper Longdon, near Rugeley - Earls of Shrewsbury

The Sutherland Arms, Stoke-on-Trent - Dukes of Sutherland

The Littleton Arms, Penkridge, Staffordshire - Lords Hatherton

The Wrottesley Arms, Wolverhampton - Lords Wrottesley

The Uxbridge Arms, Burton-on-Trent - Marquess of Anglesey

The Anglesey Arms, Burton-on-Trent - Marquess of Anglesey

Jervis Arms, Onecote - Earl St Vincent

The Sneyd Arms, Keele - Sneyd family, who used to live at Keele Hall, now part of the University of Keele

The Sneyd Arms, Sneyd Green

The Bagot Arms, Abbots Bromley, Staffordshire - Lords Bagot

Roads and Streets

Wolseley Road, Rugeley - Wolseley baronets

Anson Street, Rugeley - Earls of Lichfield

Jerningham Street, Stafford - Lords Stafford

Fitzherbert Close, Swynnerton - Lords Stafford

Ingestre Road, Stafford - Earls of Shrewsbury

Talbot Road, Rugeley - Earls of Shrewsbury

Hatherton Street, Stafford - Lords Hatherton

Paget Drive, Burntwood - Marquess of Anglesey

Paget Street, Burton-on-Trent - Marquess of Anglesey

Uxbridge Street, Burton-on-Trent - Marquess of Anglesey

Uxbridge Street, Cannock - Marquess of Anglesey

Anglesey Road, Burton-on-Trent - Marquess of Anglesey

Anglesey Street, Burton-on-Trent - Marquess of Anglesey

Leveson Road, Trentham - Dukes of Sutherland

Harrowby Street, Stafford - Earls of Harrowby

Wrottesley Road, Wolverhampton - Lords Wrottesley

Dartmouth Street, Stafford - Earls of Dartmouth

Dartmouth Street, Wolverhampton - Earls of Dartmouth

Legge Street, Wolverhampton - Earls of Dartmouth

Place Names

Austin Friars, Stafford - Lords Stafford

Granville Square, Stone - Earls Granville

Appendix 3
The Demise of the English Country House

Many people have written about the loss of country houses since the nineteenth century, a process, which accelerated after the First World War and again after the Second World War. More than 1,000 country houses were demolished in the 20th century, resulting in the permanent loss of irreplaceable historic buildings, gardens and art collections.[1] Of these, up to 400 major losses were suffered between 1919 and 1939.

England suffered more than the other Home Countries and Staffordshire suffered particularly due to a concentration of many of the catalysts for destruction outlined below.

For those who suffered the pain of losing their heritage the reasons for the destruction seemed very clear: death duties, the carnage of the First World War, which culled so many heirs, and the impact of requisitioning during the Second World War. It was somehow comforting to these people to blame external, unavoidable forces. But these were just the final nails in the coffins of country houses and a way of life that either had already died or was in its final death throes.

In fact, the decline of the English country house did not occur overnight; an early catalyst was the long-lasting agricultural depression that began ravaging the countryside in the last few decades of the 19th century. The influx of cheap corn from America - which the landed interest was no longer strong enough to keep out - led to twenty years of deep depression in the British farming industry. As a result, upper-class families who were entirely dependent on the income from their land found themselves in difficulties.[2] Land, which had never been a good financial investment compared with the stock market, had become a positively bad one and it is not surprising that many owners, finding there was no longer any political advantage in holding land, began to dispose of surplus acres - and houses. Many who had accumulated a number of country estates through marriage sold those, which were surplus to requirement. Often, the new owner kept the land but demolished the house or left it to decay. In earlier times, such secondary estates and their houses could have been justified because of the political influence they brought in their area. But now, such estates were vulnerable: for example, the Dukes of Northumberland owned Alnwick and Keilder Castle in Northumberland, Stanwick Park in Yorkshire, Syon House in Middlesex and Albury House in Surrey. When the 9th Duke needed to raise cash to pay the death duties arising from the death of the 8th Duke in 1918, the obvious choice was the Stanwick estate, which had been let after the death of the dowager duchess.

Although owning land no longer provided the power base it had done, the country house, itself, still retained some of its mystique. But it could no longer support itself just on the land surrounding it. Those families with other forms of income were in the best position to retain and maintain their country houses. In particular, rents from property development in London and elsewhere became a valuable source of income.[3] Others developed family businesses, some based upon their country houses or their estates but, like the experiences of the rest of society, not all of these ventures were a success.[4] However, any perception that one may have of aristocratic families always having had oversized houses, which they tried to cling on to whatever the consequences, is erroneous - in the second half of the 17th century, many families abandoned large Elizabethan and Jacobean houses for more compact Restoration models. The same was true in the 20th century, as oversized houses were abandoned, either for something more compact on the site or for a smaller, more convenient house elsewhere on the estate.

For centuries, country estates had been the seats of landowners who ran the country locally and through Parliament. The rise of democracy, county councils and a reformed Parliament, culminating in the emasculation of the House of Lords in 1910 - 11, [5] brought an end to the landowners' political power. With it went the political significance of the country house.

Suddenly, owners were left fumbling for a reason to continue with the expense of owning such houses. Despite their high costs and frequent inconvenience, country houses had brought power, prestige and influence. Until about 1900, anyone who wanted a part in running the nation lived in a country house. But no longer! Great Victorian houses, built for entertaining on a massive scale, were particularly vulnerable. Throughout the country, owners of every sort of house were asking themselves, "Why continue to live in a country house?"

It was a question made particularly pertinent by the aforementioned long agricultural slump, which had destroyed rents and land prices.

Those that did not sell out early found themselves sorely pressed as often they had built up large mortgages and, with rents falling, they found interest payments hard to meet. Furthermore, collapsing land prices meant that the cost of the mortgage threatened to exceed the value of their estates - heading towards the sort of situation that came to be known as 'negative equity' in one of the economic downturns in the late 20th century.

Sir William Harcourt, the Liberal Chancellor of the Exchequer, had introduced what became known as 'death duties' in 1894. These were taxes charged on a person's estate after his death. Almost inevitably, when any government identifies an easy source of revenue, tax rates increase over time and so it was with death duties and income tax.[5] Consequently, although the demands were not initially onerous, they became more deadly when combined with falling incomes and collapsing landowners' morale. This situation was further exacerbated for many families who suffered from multiple death duties during the First World War, when it was not uncommon for the head of the family, his elder son, and even that son's brother, all to have died fighting for their country. Families were often unable to cope. The families had paid a heavy price - it was as if the nation's government was not content just with family members sacrificing their lives to save the country.

Meanwhile, growing industrialisation [6] had been drawing more people from the land and into the towns, which started to spread into the countryside and began threatening the once idyllic setting of many country houses. Trentham in Staffordshire is just one example; the 4th Duke of Sutherland demolished it in 1912 because of the effects of industrial pollution from the expanding North Staffordshire conurbation centred on the Potteries' towns of Stoke-on-Trent. The Duke moved on to another of his houses.

All these factors led to massive land sales after the First World War, stimulated by a brief land-price boom, and a sharp rise in country house demolitions, as, in many cases, the purchasers were the existing tenant farmers, who already had their own farm houses. 17 houses are known to have been lost in 1926 alone. Not that all those selling up were forced to do so by dire necessity. Some had recognised that low-earning land, a large country house and increasing taxes were a drain on their resources; they therefore set about restructuring their assets. Others decided to live in idle comfort by selling up then moving overseas to less harsh tax regimes rather than face the responsibilities of being a landowner. This is a practice which continued into the 20th century not only with former landowners but high earners escaping the tax man, whose rapacious forays were not pushed back until the arrival of Margaret Thatcher, a latter-day Boudicca.

The turmoil of the Second World War and the political upheaval that followed, spelled doom for many of the houses which had survived the previous onslaught between 1919 and 1939. Requisitioning broke the thread of occupation for many families. This situation was unique to the UK - no other country effected total mobilisation during the war. Only a few houses escaped requisition, such as Erddig, which accommodated a school for a while, until, without light and with a failing water supply, it was deemed uninhabitable. Consequently, after the war finished, it is not surprising that many owners threw in the towel when faced with a badly damaged house, little money to repair it, crippling taxation and a socialist world that seemed to have no place for the country house - another heavy price to pay after the losses resulting from the First World War. Particularly vulnerable were the elderly, those with no immediate heirs, those in unfashionable (particularly early 19th century) houses and those close to big cities. Demolitions soared and, in 1955, it is said that a country house was lost every 2½ days. [7]

For those who hung on, the second half of the 1950s and 1960s saw an unexpected recovery. Agriculture boomed, driving up rents and land prices. Pictures and other works of art began to increase in value. And government grants were available to help repair many important houses. Although the rate of demolition was down on the early 1950s, it still remained high. However, the assumption that demolition was inevitable and acceptable began to be challenged. Demolishing a country house had become a matter of public concern rather than a private act.

Finally, in 1968, a new planning act forced owners to seek permission to demolish listed houses, instead of simply informing local authorities of their intention. Within a few years, the problem of demolition had faded away.

Deliberate demolition is no longer an option, but a more insidious threat has taken its place - the steady sale of the contents that have made English houses so special, principally to fund the constant cycle of repairs and maintenance that old houses need.

Despite all these attacks on their existence, England's country houses have survived albeit far fewer in number. Furthermore, as primogeniture (where the eldest keeps all) is still practised by the landed classes, houses, their contents and their settings remain intact in a way that few countries can rival in Europe. That the country has not been fought over since the Norman Conquest has also helped to preserve treasures in family hands. This has only to be compared with the art and treasure robberies perpetrated since the 18th century on the European mainland by Napoleon, the Nazis and the Russian Communists.

Country houses represent as fundamental a part of English culture as our parish churches or cathedral. The tale of destruction that is the history of the country house in the 20th century shows how vulnerable they are and reminds us that we should celebrate and cherish those that have survived, despite the profound economic and social changes in the latter part of the 19th century and during the 20th century.

However, the early part of the 21st century saw a sea change in the social make-up of the countryside, which could, in the long term, save some of the smaller country houses. This new squirearchy typically comprised couples in their thirties and forties who probably grew up in the country themselves, then made their money in the City (London) before the pull of their roots and the endless views became too strong to resist. This new landed gentry bought not just fine houses with big gardens but rolling acres of farmlands, too. The primary purpose of these acquisitions was to protect their immediate environment; the land was often rented out to existing farmers. In the 19th century, the vast majority of farmers were tenant farmers renting land off the gentry, who, with apartments in London and City incomes, had little to do with day-to-day farming. After the First World War and the aforementioned collapse of the country estate, farmers bought their own land and became owner-occupiers - in the early part of the 21st century, the trend started to reverse as many farmers released capital by selling their land and renting it back from the new owners. These new owners have often revitalised rural areas by pumping in some of their new wealth, which has re-generated the need for rural trades such as hedgelaying and thatching as well as building repair and maintenance work. Nevertheless, despite these apparently positive signs, there is still the spectre of rising interest rates and the re-emergence of negative equity, which could undermine the 'new money' investment in the countryside. There is also some evidence emerging that the love affair with the countryside is starting to wane. In summary, it is likely that the classic English country estate is doomed. Nowadays, the most valuable items on an estate are often the dilapidated farm buildings with potential for conversion into homes.

Some of Staffordshire's Lost Country Houses:

1926 - Drayton Manor, Tamworth

1926 - Tixall Hall, Nr Stafford

1912 - Trentham Hall, Nr Newcastle under Lyme

1932 - Beaudesert Hall, Nr Rugeley

19?? - Bellamour Hall, Colton, Nr Rugeley (between 1924 and 1930?)

1954 - Teddesley Hall, Penkridge

1965 - Wolseley Hall, Nr Colwich

The Demise of the English Country House
Further Notes And Connections

1. According to Giles Worsley (see Acknowledgements below), the latest research as at 2002 suggests that at least 1,200 English country houses were lost during the 20th century, a figure that might rise to 1,700 if every county was properly studied - possibly 1 in 6 of all country houses existing at the beginning of the 20th century.

2. Despite the difficulties experienced by arable farmers because of cheap imports from America, which accentuated the late 19th century agricultural depression, stock farmers gained from the low prices of animal feed.

3. Successful examples include the London estates of the Duke of Westminster in Mayfair and Belgravia, the Howard de Walden family in Marylebone (see the chapter: "The Lord Who Nearly Prevented World War II" and the Calthorpe Estate in Birmingham (Edgbaston).

4. Many landowners had grown rich on the profits from coal and iron, for example, the Littletons - see the chapter: "How To Be Comfortable In Church" and the Pagets - see the chapter: "Here Lies The Leg". However, as Giles Worsley succinctly wrote in History Today, many landowners found that they had entered a Faustian bargain as the settings of their houses were ruined by coalpits and steelworks. For another cautionary tale but one, which led to financial disaster, see the chapter: "This Land Was My Land" about Sir Charles Wolseley.

5. The British Parliament Act of 1911 cut the powers of the House of Lords to interfere with and retard House of Commons legislation, asserting the supremacy of the House of Commons. The origins of this Act stemmed from a clash between the Liberal government and the Lords over the so-called 'People's Budget' of 1909 of David Lloyd George, the Liberal Chancellor of the Exchequer. In 1908, Lloyd George had introduced the Old Age Pensions Act that provided between 1s (5p) and 5s (25p) a week to people over 70. To pay for these pensions, Lloyd George had to raise government revenues by an additional £16 million a year. Consequently, the 1909 budget included the following increases in taxation to fund this new requirement: people on lower incomes were to pay 9d (3¾p) in the pound, those on annual incomes of over £3,000 had to pay 1s 2d (c6p) in the pound

and a new supertax of 6d (2½ p) in the pound for those earning £5,000 a year. Other proposed measures included an increase in death duties on the estates of the rich and the introduction of a land tax based on the ideas of the American tax reformer, Henry George. This last proposal would have had a major effect on large landowners, many of whom were Conservative peers. As they had a large majority in the Lords, they made it clear that they would block the proposals. Lloyd George's reaction was to portray the nobility as men who were using their privileged position to stop the poor from receiving their old age pension. The Liberals used the ensuing unpopularity of the Lords when they called and won the General Election of 1910. Carried by the wave of popularity, the Liberal government then used this as a mandate to push through the 1911 Parliament Act, which drastically cut the powers of the Lords. They were no longer allowed to prevent the passage of 'money bills' and it also restricted their ability to delay other legislation to three sessions of parliament. The bill also changed the maximum length of time between general elections from seven years to five and provided for Members of Parliament to be paid. The bill was passed despite initial opposition from the House of Lords, which evaporated when the Liberal Prime Minister, Henry Asquith, appealed to George V, who agreed that, if necessary, he would create 250 new Liberal peers to remove the Conservative majority in the Lords. The Conservative Lords backed down but they had achieved one victory - the land tax proposal was quietly dropped. The 1911 Act was amended in 1949 to reduce the power of the Lords further by cutting the time they could delay the passing of bills from two years to one year.

6. Despite industrialisation encroaching on their privacy, some of the brighter members of the land-owning classes took advantage of the wealth created and joined up with the business world. They also married into the 'new money'! However, this was by no means a new phenomenon - landowners had been marrying the daughters of the new men from the city since at least the 16th century. But, post-industrialisation, the new men began to obtain the upper hand and, by the mid 19th century, people were no longer expected to cut all ties with business before being accepted as a member of the upper classes.

7. John Harris – 'No Voice From The Hall: Early Memories of a Country House Snooper' - see Acknowledgements below.

The Demise of the English Country House
Acknowledgements

Binney, Marcus (1984), *Our Vanishing Heritage,* Arlington Books; ISBN 0851406351

Girouard, Mark (1979), *Life in the English Country House,* Yale University Press; ISBN 0300022735

Harris, John (1998), *No Voice From The Hall: Early Memories of a Country House Snooper,* John Murray; ISBN 0719555671

Worsley, Giles (2002), *England's Lost Houses,* Aurum Press; ISBN 1854108204

Worsley, Giles (August 2002), *History Today Ltd*

Wikipedia website

Daily Telegraph

Further Reading

Hoskins, W.G. (1955), *The Making of the English Landscape*, Hodder & Stoughton; ISBN 0340770201

Appendix 4
The Cliffords

For many of the Cliffords scattered around the world, their common ancestor is said to be a Norman called Pons, who came over to England in 1066 with William the Conqueror.

Pons settled in Herefordshire and his descendants soon became 'Marcher Lords'. [1] The surname comes from Clifford in Herefordshire, the site of one of their string of castles, in which they held court. Although one of the roles given to them by their kings was to contain the Welsh princes, their first loyalty was to themselves. They frequently changed sides in the baronial wars during the reigns of Stephen, John and Henry III but such manoeuvrings did not always save them. However, it was the death in 1285 of Roger Clifford, sole Justiciar of Wales, which triggered Edward I's final conquest of Wales.

Robert Clifford, 1st Baron Clifford, took part in the Battle of Falkirk in 1298 that saw King Edward I's decisive victory over William Wallace and was rewarded with the governorship of Nottingham Castle. However, he was later killed at the Battle of Bannockburn in 1314.

The Cliffords enhanced their fortune by frequently marrying wealthy heiresses. One such marriage resulted in a move to Westmoreland where, again, they became Marcher Lords but now with the Scots as opponents. A new building programme resulted in castles at Brough, Brougham, Appleby, Pendragon and Skipton.

The mediaeval Cliffords travelled extensively as pilgrims or crusaders. However, like all families, not all the Cliffords were pleasant people. A particularly bloodthirsty member was John, 9th Lord Clifford, known as Blackfaced Clifford amongst other epithets such as Bloody and Butcher; he was a leader of the Lancastrian forces in the Wars of the Roses. His father, Thomas, 8th Lord Clifford, had been killed in 1455 at St Albans in the first battle of these wars; John was killed in 1461 at the last battle of the Wars of the Roses at Towton. However, he had already incurred the wrath of the Yorkists at the Battle of Wakefield on 31 December 1460 where he is alleged to have cut off the head of the Duke of York's corpse after which the head was decked with a paper crown and impaled above the gates of York. The Duke of York's sons, Edward IV and Richard III, were never to forget this deed and, after the Yorkist victory at the Battle of Towton on 29 March 1461, the defeated Lancastrians suffered attainders and forfeitures of estates of unsurpassed severity. Although clemency was later shown to some nobles, no mercy was shown to the Cliffords. It was not until the reign of the Tudor King Henry VIII that their lands and castles were restored. Henry, 11th Lord Clifford, is said to have been brought up with the future King Henry VIII, who created him Earl of Cumberland on 18 June 1525. Henry stood by the king in the religious and political troubles leading to and after the separation of the Church in England from Rome. As a reward for his loyalty, the Earl of Cumberland was granted the newly dissolved abbey of Bolton together with its Skipton possessions and nine manors in Yorkshire. The 5th and last Earl of Cumberland died in 1643. Bolton Abbey eventually passed by marriage to the Cavendish family, later Dukes of Devonshire.

The barony of Clifford of Chudleigh was created in 1672 for Thomas Clifford, a descendant of Walter de Clifford of Clifford Castle. [2,3] Thomas held the position of Lord High Treasurer in 1672-3 but, being a Roman Catholic, was forced to resign by the Test Act. [4] However, more importantly, he was a member of the CABAL at Charles II's court, namely **C**lifford, **A**rlington, **B**uckingham, **A**shley and **L**auderdale, which operated from 1667 to 1672. Their initials coincidentally spelt 'cabal', a word whose definition is "a number of persons united in some close design, usually to promote their private views and interests in church or state by intrigue". However, the members did not live up to the definition and the 'cabal' fell apart.

Another Thomas Clifford, the 4th son of Hugh, the 3rd Lord Clifford of Chudleigh, was born in London on 22 August 1732. His father had died five months earlier on 26 March 1732 at Ugbrooke, the family seat in Devon. Hugh and his wife, Elizabeth (née Blount) had six children, two of whom died in infancy. Elizabeth died in Paris 46 years after Hugh. Thomas married Barbara Aston, younger daughter of Walter, 4th Lord Aston of Forfar, of Tixall Hall near Stafford.[5]

One of the most interesting members of the Clifford family is Lady Anne Clifford, Countess of Pembroke (1590-1676). Anne was born at Skipton Castle during the reign of Elizabeth I. She was the third and only surviving child of

George Clifford, 3rd Earl of Cumberland, and his wife Margaret Russell. When she was 15, her father died. She was upset to find she did not inherit her father's vast estate, which went to the Earl's brother. The Earl of Cumberland had not recognised the strength and determination of his only surviving child. From that moment, Anne's mission in life was to obtain what she regarded as her inheritance. Her second husband, Philip Herbert, Earl of Pembroke, not only supported her claim but also provided her with two things of importance; he employed Inigo Jones to restore the family home, and gave Anne inspiration for her later building efforts. Eventually, in 1643, her endeavours paid off - she inherited her father's estate. She spent the next 26 years rebuilding churches and castles. Skipton, Pendragon, Appleby, Brough and Brougham Castles were restored to their former glory. As a devout Christian she built and restored churches and almshouses.

The Cliffords
Further Notes and Connections

1. Put simply, the Marcher Lords were the Anglo-Norman barons who held lands in the border regions between England and Wales and between England and Scotland. However, real situation was far more complex. For example, the authority of the Marcher Lords was far different from that enjoyed by English barons. The right to crenellate (i.e. build castles or fortify existing structures) was jealously guarded by the sovereign within England. This right was only granted to men deemed trustworthy. Yet the Marcher Lords could build and fortify castles at will. They could also wage war on their own, a right definitely not available to their English counterparts. Yet many of the Marcher Lords also owned large estates in England, where many spent much of their time.

2. The Chudleigh and Boscombe lines began with Sir Lewis Clifford Kt (1364-1404), a younger son of Roger, 5th Baron Clifford. Sir Lewis incurred disfavour as a Lollard - see Appendix 7: Dissolution of the Monasteries and The Reformation.

3. Sir Walter de Clifford's daughter was the 'Fair Rosamund', the most favoured mistress of Henry II. She died in 1176, possibly from poisoning.

4. The several Test Acts were a series of English penal laws that imposed various civil disabilities on Roman Catholics and nonconformists.

5. For more information on the Staffordshire connections of the Astons and Cliffords, see the chapters: "What's In A Family Name" and "Colton's Lost Country House".

The Cliffords
Acknowledgements

Clifford, Hugh (1987), *The House of Clifford*, Phillimore & Co; ISBN 0850336341

Weir, Alison (1995), *Lancaster & York: The Wars of the Roses*, Pimlico: ISBN 0712666745

Huguenot Society of South Africa, http://www.geocities.com/Heartland/ Valley/8140/begin-e.htm (accessed 2004)

The Columbia Encyclopedia, http://www.bartleby.com/65/cl/CliffrdCh.html (accessed 2004)

Wikipedia, http://en.wikipedia.org/wiki/Thomas_Clifford%2C_1st_Baron_ Clifford_of_Chudleigh (accessed 2004)

Clifford family http://www.tudorplace.com.ar/CLIFFORD.htm

Appendix 5
The Blounts

When researching into the family history of aristocratic Staffordshire families, people bearing the Blount family name appear frequently. The family name has also been lent to several place names around England, including Blount's Green on the outskirts of Uttoxeter, Staffordshire, and Barton Blount in Derbyshire, where the 4th Baron Mountjoy was born and buried. Like many of the old aristocratic names, it is not pronounced as it is spelt; the correct pronunciation being 'Blunt'.

From my investigations, tracing the family from the 13/14th century is relatively straightforward; before then, there seem to be some arguments over the family origins. Some people have claimed to show descent from Norman families bearing the name 'de Guisnes', one pedigree showing the Blounts to be descendants of a Rudolph (Ralph) de Guisnes. Others have disputed such claims, one going as far as saying, "... there seems to be no evidence to connect any early Blounts with the counts of Guisnes. This sort of thing, making an early Norman thug or post-conquest parvenu into a continental count's son (pick a count at random), was a common unfounded pedigree embellishment". He also goes on to say, "... most Americans, who descend from Blounts, descend from the Blounts of the stock of the Lords Mountjoy; their ancestry is not known before the mid fourteenth century". [1]

An early example of a Blount associated with Staffordshire is a Hugh le Blount, who is known to have held land in Penkridge, Staffordshire, and in Essex around 1300. He was a frequent representative for Essex in the parliaments of Edward I and Edward II.

Another early Blount associated with Staffordshire was Sir Walter Blount Kt, who was appointed constable of Tutbury Castle [2] for life by John of Gaunt, Duke of Lancaster, in January 1372/73. Sir Walter was the son of Sir John Blount and Isoude (Isolda) de Mountjoy, the origin of Mountjoy name taken by Sir Walter's grandson, when he became the 1st Baron Mountjoy. Sir Walter was killed at the Battle of Shrewsbury in 1403, fighting for Henry IV against Henry 'Hotspur' Percy's forces.

The 1st Baron Mountjoy was to play a significant role in mediaeval politics as Lord High Treasurer to Edward IV. His second marriage was to Anne, Duchess of Buckingham, widow of Humphrey Stafford, 1st Duke of Buckingham.[3]

The previously mentioned 4th Baron Mountjoy, William Blount, was famous as a scholar and patron of learning. He was a pupil of Erasmus [4], who called him 'inter nobiles doctissimus'. He also signed the letter to the Pope conveying Henry VIII's threat to repudiate the papal supremacy unless his divorce from Catherine of Aragon was granted. Mountjoy, who was one of the wealthiest English nobles of his time, died in 1534. His son, Charles, 5th Baron Mountjoy, was also a patron of learning.

Another branch of the Blounts lived around Mamble and Sodington, Worcestershire, and at Mawley Hall, near Cleobury Mortimer, Shropshire. Although in different counties all these places lie close to one another being on opposite sides of the border separating the two counties. The 1st Blount Baronet of Sodington was yet another Sir Walter! His daughter, Eleanor, married Sir Walter Aston, 3rd Lord Aston of Forfar.[4] The 6th Blount baronet, also called Walter, married his cousin, Mary Aston, daughter of the 5th Lord Aston of Tixall Hall near Stafford. [5,6]

The Blounts
Further Notes and Connections

1. The Peerage.com article on 'Mountjoy' provides a conservative presentation of this lineage of the 'Blounts' - see Acknowledgements below.

2. Tutbury Castle has played an important role in English history on several occasions. It was a major centre for John of Gaunt (after Ghent where he was born), Duke of Lancaster, who was the 4th son of Edward III and the father of Henry IV. Tutbury Castle later came into the hands of the Earls of Shrewsbury during which time it housed Mary, Queen of Scots, for part of her period of imprisonment before she was executed at Fotheringhay Castle. For more on the Earls of Shrewsbury, see the chapter: "The Premier Earls".

3. For more information on the Stafford family, see the chapter: "Titles Move In Mysterious Ways".

4. Erasmus was one of the great figures of the Renaissance. He was a Dutch humanist, who taught throughout Europe. An ordained priest of the Roman Catholic Church, he combined vast learning with a fine style, keen humour, moderation and tolerance. Although he remained a loyal Catholic and opposed the Protestant Reformation, he championed church reform. He became a bitter opponent of Martin Luther and, in 'On the Freedom of the Will', he denounced Luther's position on predestination. For more information on the Protestant Reformation, see Appendix 7: Dissolution of the Monasteries and The Reformation.

5. For more information on the Aston family, see the chapter: "What's In A Family Name?".

6. The abbreviated family pedigrees at the end of this chapter show some of the family connections between the Blounts and other Staffordshire-related families.

The Blounts
Acknowledgements

Lundy, Darryl website http://www.thepeerage.com/ (accessed 2003 - 2005)

Further Reading

Taylor, Nathaniel & Todd Farmerie (1998), *Notes on the Ancestry of Sancha de Ayala,* New England Historical and Genealogical Register (New England Historical and Genealogical Society, Boston), 152:41. Sancha de Ayala married Sir Walter Blount, who was killed at the Battle of Shrewsbury, 21 July 1403.

BLOUNTS OF SODINGTON: SOME CONNECTIONS WITH STAFFORDSHIRE FAMILIES AND OTHERS

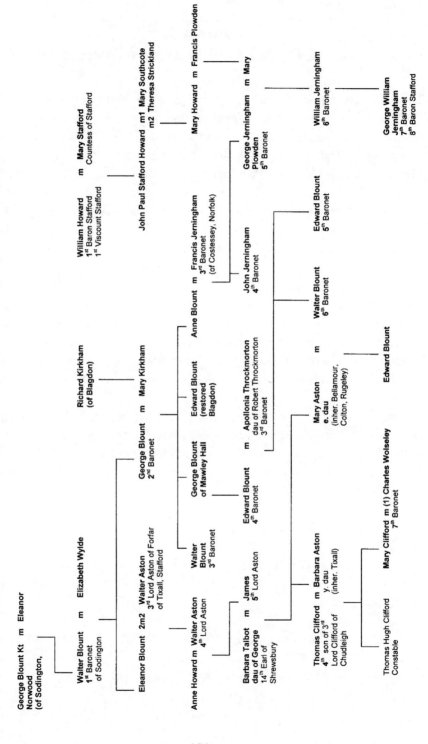

Appendix 6
Great Offices of State of England

There are nine Great Officers of State of England: some are either vested in the Monarch, are obsolete, have become sinecure or are only fulfilled during official events such as coronations and trials of Peers. They are listed below in rank order, and, as such, follow the Royal Family and the Archbishop of Canterbury in the Order of Precedence:

Lord High Steward, Lord High Chancellor, Lord High Treasurer, Lord President of the Council, Lord Privy Seal, Lord Great Chamberlain, Lord High Constable, Earl Marshal and Lord High Admiral.

Nowadays, the Lord High Steward and the Lord High Constable are called out of abeyance for coronations and other rare occasions. The Lord Great Chamberlain is the holder of a hereditary ceremonial post concerned with the sovereign's attendance at Parliament and great state occasions, such as the lying-in state of a recently deceased sovereign and the coronation of the new one. The history of the holders of this post is a story in itself. [1]

In past times, one or more of the above posts have been held by members of families with Staffordshire connections, some examples of which are given below and, in some cases, are mentioned elsewhere in this book:

Lord High Steward at coronations:

- Earl Talbot (1761 - George III)

- 1st Marquess of Anglesey (1821 - George IV)

Lord Presidents

- 2nd Earl Gower, Granville Leveson-Gower (1767 - 1779, 1783 - 1784)

- 1st Earl of Harrowby, Dudley Ryder (1812 -1827)

- 2nd Earl Granville, Granville George Leveson-Gower (1852 -1854, 1855 - 1858, 1859 - 1866)

Lord Privy Seal

- 1st Baron Paget, William Paget (1555 -1571)

- 1st Earl of Dartmouth, William Legge (1713 - 1714)

- 2nd Baron Gower, John Leveson-Gower (1742 - 1743)

- 1st Earl Gower, John Leveson-Gower (1744 - 1755)

- 2nd Earl Gower, Granville Leveson-Gower (1755 - 1757)

- 2nd Earl of Dartmouth, William Legge (1775 - 1782)

- 1st Marquess of Stafford, Granville Leveson-Gower (1784 - 1794)

- 2nd Earl of Harrowby, Dudley Ryder (1855 -1858)

- 3rd Earl of Harrowby, Dudley Ryder (1885 -1886)

Lord Great Chamberlain

- 2nd Duke of Buckingham, Henry Stafford (1483 - Richard III's coronation)

Lord High Constable

- 5th Earl of Stafford, Edmund Stafford (1399 - 1403)

- 1st Duke of Buckingham, Humphrey Stafford (1403 - 1460)

- 2nd Duke of Buckingham, Henry Stafford (1460 - 1483)

- 3rd Duke of Buckingham, Edward Stafford (1485 - 1521)

At this point, the office was merged into the crown and only revived for coronations.

Earl Marshal

- 6th Earl of Shrewsbury, George Talbot (1572 - 1590)

Great Officers of State of England
Further Notes and Connections

1.   The office of Lord Great Chamberlain is a hereditary one, and was originally held by Robert Malet, a son of one of the leading companions of William the Conqueror. In 1133, however, Henry I declared Malet's estates and titles forfeit, and awarded the office of Lord Great Chamberlain to Aubrey de Vere, whose son was created Earl of Oxford. Thereafter, the Earls of Oxford held the title almost continuously until 1526, with a few intermissions due to the forfeiture of some Earls for treason. In 1526, however, the 14th Earl of Oxford died, leaving his aunts as his female heirs. The earldom was inherited by a more distant heir-male, his second cousin. Henry VIII then declared that the office belonged to the Crown, and was not transmitted along with the earldom. The Sovereign appointed the 15th and 16th Earls to the office, but the appointments were deemed for life and were uninheritable. Then, Mary I ruled that the Earls of Oxford were indeed entitled to the office of Lord Great Chamberlain on an hereditary basis. John de Vere, the 15th Earl of Oxford, married Elizabeth Trussell, heiress of Edward Trussell, a substantial landowner around Stafford. See also the chapter: "How To Be Comfortable In Church".

The 16th, 17th and 18th Earls of Oxford held the office of Lord Great Chamberlain on a hereditary basis until 1625, when the 18th Earl died, leaving a distant relative as heir to the earldom. However, there was a closer female relative and the House of Lords eventually ruled that the office should pass to Robert Bertie, the son of Mary de Vere and Peregrine Bertie, 12th Baron Willoughby de Eresby. Robert became the 13th Baron Willoughby de Eresby and later the 1st Earl of Lindsey. Mary de Vere was daughter of John de Vere, 16th Earl of Oxford and aunt of the 18th Earl. The 19th Earl of Oxford was only a second cousin to the 18th Earl.

The office of Lord Great Chamberlain remained vested in the Earls of Lindsey, who later became Dukes of Ancaster and Kesteven. However, when the 4th Duke of Ancaster and Kesteven died in 1779, he left two sisters as female heirs, and an uncle as a male heir.

The uncle became 5th Duke, but, this time, the House of Lords ruled that the two sisters were jointly Lord Great Chamberlain, and could appoint a deputy to fulfil its functions. The barony of Willoughby de Eresby went into abeyance between the two sisters, but George III terminated the abeyance and granted the title to the elder sister, Priscilla. The younger sister later married the first Marquess of Cholmondeley. The office of Lord Great Chamberlain, however, was divided between Priscilla and her younger sister, Georgiana. Priscilla's share was eventually split between two of her granddaughters, and has been split several more times since then. By contrast, Georgiana's share has been inherited by a single male heir each time; that individual has in each case been the Marquess of Cholmondeley, a title created for Georgiana's husband.

At any one time, a single person actually exercises the office of Lord Great Chamberlain. The various individuals who hold fractions of the Lord Great Chamberlainship are technically each *Joint Hereditary Lord Great Chamberlain*, and the right to exercise the office for a given reign rotates proportionately to the fraction of the office held. For instance, the Marquesses of Cholmondeley hold one-half of the office, and may therefore exercise the office or appoint a deputy every alternate reign. A *Deputy Lord Great Chamberlain* is a person exercising the office who is *not* personally a co-heir to the office; historically these have been sons or husbands of co-heirs as the office has never been exercised by a female, females having been forbidden to sit in the Lords until the present reign.

Appendix 7
Dissolution of the Monasteries and The Reformation

The 15th and 16th centuries were a period of religious turmoil throughout Europe and people started to question the power of the Pope and the Catholic Church. It should be understood that what has become known as the Protestant Reformation was a movement, which began as a series of attempts to reform the Roman Catholic Church. However, it ended in division and the establishment of several other Christian churches, most importantly the Lutheran Church, Reformed churches, and Anabaptists. An understanding of this turmoil is necessary to put the dissolution of the monasteries into context. Contrary to what many people believe, the dissolution was not an anti-Catholic act - Henry VIII still considered himself to be a Catholic.

The first big step in the process of Reformation was in 1517 when Martin Luther, a monk from Wittenburg in Germany, began criticising the power and corruption of the Pope and the Catholic Church. He attacked the Pope for pardoning people's sins in exchange for money. Luther thought that it was immoral for the Pope's agents (pardoners) to travel all over Europe selling these letters of indulgence. Luther also criticised the Pope for not allowing the Bible to be translated into other languages. Luther argued that, as the vast majority of people could not read Latin, they had to rely on what the priest told them was in the Bible.

Luther's views on the Church were not new. In the 14th century, John Wycliffe and his Lollard [1] followers had said similar things in England.

Pope Leo X ordered Martin Luther to stop inciting trouble. This attempt to keep Luther quiet had the opposite effect. Luther started issuing statements about other issues such as questioning the infallibility of the Pope: Luther was convinced that Leo X was wrong to sell indulgences; therefore, Luther argued, the Pope could not possibly be infallible. In 1521, orders were given for Luther to be arrested. However, Luther had many supporters in Germany and some of these people helped to save his life by hiding him in a castle. While Luther was there he translated the Bible into German. It was not long before copies of

Luther's Bible were being read by people all over Germany.

Martin Luther was more successful than John Wycliffe in gaining support for reforming the Church. His supporters became known as Protestants because they were protesting against the way the Church was governed. Luther's ideas also spread to other countries. Gradually large numbers of people living in England, the Netherlands (now Holland and Belgium), Switzerland and the Scandinavian countries began to call themselves Lutherans or Protestants. Protestants were no longer willing to accept the authority of the Pope. They argued that people needed to read the Bible if they wanted to find out how God wanted them to behave.

Henry VIII disagreed with Luther's proclamations, as he feared that criticism of the Church might encourage people to criticise the monarchy. At the time, it was believed that Wycliffe's attacks on the Pope had been partly responsible for the Peasants' Revolt in 1381. In 1521, Henry wrote a book attacking Luther's views on the Church. As a reward for Henry's loyalty, the Pope gave him the title 'Defender of the Faith'.

Henry's opinions about the power of the Pope changed after he was denied permission to divorce Catherine of Aragon. In 1534, Henry made himself head of the Church in England in place of the Pope. Although Henry continued to persecute English Protestants, he was now also hostile to those who remained loyal to the Pope. He was particularly worried that he did not have the full support of the monks and nuns in England.

At the same time, Henry's government needed money, but knew it would be unpopular to demand new taxes from Parliament. It was, therefore, unfortunate for the monasteries that this coincided with Henry's concern about the loyalty of the monasteries in England.

The idea of dissolving the monasteries was conceived by Thomas Cromwell in about 1534, but the plan was not put into practice until 1536 after Henry VIII had appointed him Vicar-General of the English Church in 1535. Thomas Cromwell sent out his agents to conduct a commission of enquiry into the character and value of all ecclesiastical property in the kingdom. Overtly, they were reformers, exercising the new powers accorded to the Crown by the Act of Supremacy: "from time to time to visit, repress, redress, reform, order, correct, restrain and amend all such errors, heresies, abuses, offences, contempts and enormities . . . which ought or may be lawfully reformed." The results of this enquiry not only provided Henry VIII with much valuable information on the wealth of the religious establishments but also evidence of corruption and immorality in England's monasteries, which he required to justify his future actions. Such evidence was not hard to find, for by the 16th century many of the religious houses had long since lost their sense of purpose. Some, as landlords, oppressed the local population with exorbitant rents. Heavy debts encumbered other religious establishments that had been poorly managed. Even so, the monasteries still owned well over a quarter of all the cultivated land in England.

The information gathered, whether or not it was embellished, gave Henry the excuse to begin in 1536 what is now known as The Dissolution of the Monasteries. It is not known exactly how many establishments were dissolved.[2] However, the smaller monasteries were dealt with first, perhaps with the objective of minimising resistance or avoiding too much outcry. At this juncture, it should be pointed out that Cardinal Wolsey, during his period as Lord Chancellor (1515 - 1529), had already suppressed several very small religious houses to finance the establishment of two colleges at Ipswich and Oxford.[3]

Statutes of 1536 dissolved 327 establishments, transferred their estates to the Crown, and pensioned off the displaced monks.[4] However, these pensions did not allow for the rapid inflation that was taking place in England at that time and within a few years most monks and nuns, who did not find other employment, were in a state of extreme poverty.

The attack on the greater monasteries began with the looting of the treasures of Bury St Edmunds early in 1538 and ended in March 1540 with the closure of Waltham Abbey.[5] The friaries were also suppressed, as in the years that followed were collegiate churches, chantries, hospitals, almshouses and schools, which until then had been largely run by the Church. The church at Penkridge was one example of a collegiate church in Staffordshire.

In the five years between 1536 and 1540, all the monasteries in England and Wales were dissolved. The monks were dispossessed, given pensions and scattered. Overall, around 5,000 monks, 1,600 friars, and 2,000 nuns were pensioned off. Such munificence did not apply to the thousands of servants, who depended on the monasteries for welfare; there was no pension for them, they simply joined the ranks of 'sturdy beggars'.

Once a monastery had surrendered to the commissioners it was ransacked, so that the Crown could maximise its profits from the plunder and, except where the building acted as the parish church, then blighted in order to prevent the monks re-occupying it.

Sales of the goods, chattels and properties started almost immediately. Some of the rich landed families of later years began to accumulate their estates in this way. In Staffordshire, this included the Levesons (later Leveson-Gowers) and the Pagets.

Many of the monasteries went for bargain prices because the market was flooded with properties as Henry VIII desperately tried to finance his wars, in particular, with France. Nevertheless, this grand dispersal earned the Crown the loyalty of the existing landed gentry, who were able to increase their estates, and members of the merchant middle class, who seized their chance to become landed gentry themselves. The successful bidders or grantees now had their own sound economic reasons for supporting and maintaining the break with Rome.[6]

Of the religious establishments in Staffordshire, Burton Abbey was the largest Benedictine [7] monastery. Trentham Priory was an Augustinian foundation, as was Lilleshall Abbey, just over the Staffordshire border into Shropshire. Dieulacres Abbey, near Leek, North Staffordshire, belonged to the Cistercian order.

Following dissolution, Burton Abbey went to the Paget [8] family, later Marquesses of Anglesey, Trentham Priory to the Leveson-Gowers [9], later the Dukes of Sutherland and Earls Granville, and Dieulacres Abbey [10] to Sir Ralph Bagnall from Newcastle-under-Lyme. The Leveson-Gowers also obtained Lilleshall Abbey.

Amongst these original purchasers, Sir Ralph Bagnall was unusual in that he chose not to emulate other merchants whose purchase of abbeys enabled them to set up as provincial grandees, with imposing stately mansions and vast parks. Sir Ralph sold off his estates piecemeal, largely to his tenants whose ancestors first leased the farms from Dieulacres. Consequently, Leek developed as a community in the seventeenth century without either an over-mighty lord directing its affairs or a powerful Anglican clergy.

In 1536, Henry VIII had given permission for an English translation of the Bible to be published in England. He also ordered that a copy of this Bible should be placed in every church in his kingdom. He still considered himself to be a Catholic, but by taking this action, he began to move the Church in the direction of Protestantism.

Protestantism did not start to take hold until after Henry VIII died in 1547. As Edward VI was too young to rule, his uncle, Edward Seymour, Duke of Somerset, took over the running of the country. The Duke of Somerset was a Protestant and he soon began to make changes to the Church of England such as the introduction of an English Prayer Book and the decision to allow members of the clergy to get married. Also, attempts were made to destroy those aspects of religion that were associated with the Catholic Church, for example, the removal of stained-glass windows in churches and the destruction of religious wall-paintings.

But Edward VI's death, at the age of 16, after only six years on the throne cut short the Protestants' ascendancy. After the unsuccessful attempt to put Lady Jane Grey on the throne, Edward was succeeded by his half-sister, Mary, now better known as Bloody Mary for her brutal suppression of the Protestant faith. Mary, who had been brought up as a Roman Catholic, declared that the Pope was the only true head of the Church. This was followed by the execution of Thomas Cranmer, the Archbishop of Canterbury and other Protestants who refused to accept the Pope as head of the Church. People were also punished if they were found reading bibles that had been printed in the English language. However, the most common cause of heresy concerned transubstantiation. Catholics believed that the bread and wine used at communion became the body and blood of Jesus Christ. Protestants, who refused to believe this miracle happened during communion, were in danger of being executed.

Mary reigned for five years before being succeeded by Elizabeth, her half-sister. Elizabeth, who was a Protestant, proceeded to reverse all of Mary's moves to make England a Catholic country again.

Following the brief Catholic reaction during Mary's reign, a consensus developed during the reign of Elizabeth I, from which we may date the origins of Anglicanism. The compromise was uneasy, and was still capable of veering between extremes but compared with the bloody and chaotic state of affairs in contemporary France [11], it was relatively successful. Despite the success of the

Catholic Counter-Reformation on the Continent and the growth of a Puritan party dedicated to further Protestant reform, it was not until the 1640s that England underwent religious strife comparable with that which her neighbours had suffered some generations before.

Dissolution of the Monasteries and the Reformation
Further Notes and Connections

1. 'Lollard' was a continental term of abuse for a religious zealot whose attitudes appeared to be suspect. The most important Lollards were a group of knights who were part of Edward III's court. These included Sir William Neville, Sir John Montague and Sir William Beauchamp, with sympathetic support and active protection from the Black Prince and John of Gaunt (at least from 1371 to 1382), which reflected traditional noble anti-clericalism. With the help of the English monarchy, the Pope and the Catholic Church crushed the Lollards as a mainstream movement. However, it survived as a sturdy underground movement, despite the putting to death by burning of several of its adherents - in the 15th century, its level-headed piety appealed to the self-made Bible-reading craftsmen, who had little time for the official and popular pieties of pilgrimage and devotions to images and relics.

2. At least 650 monasteries and over 850 monastic houses in England and Wales were dissolved in the process now known as "The Dissolution of the Monasteries".

3. The life of Cardinal Wolsey is one of the great cautionary tales of Henry VIII's reign; like his protégé, Thomas Cromwell, Wolsey rose and fell by the whim of a contrary and contradictory king. Wolsey and Henry became close friends, or as close as one could be to a king. Both men were determined to leave their mark upon history but while Henry preferred costly wars and grandiloquent diplomacy, Wolsey was committed to financial and judicial reform in England and English-arbitrated European peace. Wolsey was always a churchman though this should not imply ignorance of the material world. He was determined to gain his own fortune, thus cementing his rise from obscurity. He also possessed a great legal mind and a shrewd understanding of international affairs. He combined these attributes with his earlier spiritual training to dominate both the secular and spiritual aspects of English life. Although Wolsey had been worldly and his private life had not been stainless, he had always been a Catholic. His last days were embittered by the news that the king intended to suppress the

two colleges, at Ipswich and Oxford, which he had founded with such care, although it must be remembered they had been financed by the suppression of some religious establishments. The college at Ipswich perished, but Christ Church, originally known as Cardinal's College, survived.

4. In 1536, a new government department, the Court of Augmentations, was created to administer the new Crown revenues from the dissolved monasteries and it paid pensions to the monks and nuns even after most of the former monastery lands had been sold by crown; however, by 1552, about half of the pensions were in arrears. In 1547, the Court was amalgamated with the Court of General Surveyors and the Exchequer absorbed both in 1554.

5. Sir Thomas Howard, 1st Baron Howard de Walden and, later, 1st Earl of Suffolk, who was Lord Treasurer to James I, built Audley End on the site of Waltham Abbey. Audley End was so huge that James I is said to have remarked that it was too large for a king but not for Sir Thomas. In fact, it was so unmanageable that about half of it was demolished in the early 18th century. Nonetheless, this still left a very substantial mansion. The house later passed to Sir John Griffin Griffin, who became the 4th Baron Howard de Walden. For more on the Howard de Waldens and Sir Thomas Howard, see the chapter: "The Lord Who Nearly Prevented World War II" and the accompanying Further Notes and Connections.

6. In his 'English Social History', G M Trevelyan argued that, if Henry had not been bankrupt from his foolish wars in France, he might never have dissolved the monasteries at all. However, history has shown that oppressed people do not stay oppressed forever - it is only a matter of time before change, which itself may not be any better.

7. Because of a reputation for corruption and slackness, which both the Benedictine monasteries and the Augustinian priories earned, many religious men sought for a return to a stricter way of life. As a result, the Savigniac and Cistercian orders (The Reformed Orders) were founded in France. As the Savigniac monks soon slipped into old ways, the Pope forcibly merged the order with the Cistercians. Although the Cistercian monasteries of Staffordshire played a significant role in the development of agriculture and industry, particularly in the clearing of wasteland and the production of wool, they soon fell back into the ways of their unreformed brothers. Dieulacres Abbey and Combermere Abbey, over the border in Cheshire, had particularly

unsavoury reputations.

8.   For more on the Pagets, see the chapter: "Here Lies The Leg".

9.   The involvement of the Leveson-Gowers in local and national affairs is discussed in more detail in the chapters: "A Family Of Influence" and "The Earl Who Washed His Own Socks".

10.   In 1221, as an act of piety on returning from the Crusade, the 6th Earl of Chester, Ranulph de Blondeville built Dieulacres Abbey. He then endowed the Abbey with his manor and forests at Swythamley. The Swythamley Park estate was then held by the Abbey until it was dissolved in 1538. The estate was granted to William Trafford from Cheshire, whose descendants owned it until 1831, when it was sold to William Brocklehurst, a silk manufacture from Manchester. His nephew, Philip Lancaster Brocklehurst, inherited it in 1859 - See the chapter: "The North Staffordshire Wallabies".

11.   From 1562 to 1598, France was split by religious wars: the Protestant minorities were cruelly persecuted by powerful Catholic nobles as well as wealthy bishops. News of the St. Bartholomew's Day Massacre in 1572 shocked Elizabeth I's court in Protestant England. Many French fled into exile. Eventually, the Protestant Henri IV came to the French throne in 1589, but he was forced to adopt the Catholic faith. Henri's Edict of Nantes in 1598 ended the wars by offering the Protestants a few towns where they could defend themselves. The great majority of French people, in the North as elsewhere, remained Catholic. Henri was followed by Louis XIII, who was strongly influenced by Cardinal Richelieu, probably best known for the portrayal of him in 'The Three Musketeers' by Alexandre Dumas. Louis XIII was succeeded by the 'Sun King', the autocratic French king Louis XIV, who was convinced of the principle "One faith, one king, one law." He was the most powerful king in Europe, and a Catholic. Many of his wars had a religious edge to them, "Protestants vs. Catholics" - his constant enemies were the Protestant English, Dutch, and some of the German princes. He gave support to English Catholics, and made the secret Treaty of Dover with Charles II in 1670 to restore Roman Catholicism to England. Later, he supported the cause of Catholic James II, who was deposed in 1688, in the 'Glorious Revolution', and also that of the Scottish Catholic princes. Personally, in middle age, Louis XIV became more religious - though it did not stop him keeping several mistresses. Encouraged by his Catholic clergy, including influential Archbishop Fenelon of Cambrai, Louis sent royal troops on raids to force French Protestants

- known as 'Huguenots' - into mass conversions to Catholicism. The king ordered "no violence", and it is possible that he was not aware of the excesses of his over-zealous officers. Finally in 1685, he revoked the Edict of Nantes, which by then gave little protection to French Protestants. He banned the practice of any religion except Roman Catholicism in France. More than half a million Protestants fled the country after more horrible massacres by royal soldiers. The persecution of the Protestants was popular with the Catholic bishops, and with many French people. But French philosopher Voltaire described it as "one of the greatest disasters that ever afflicted France". Without the Huguenots, the army and navy were much weaker, and French industry lost many of its most highly skilled craftsmen, who set up business in exile, to the benefit of France's enemies in England, Germany and the Netherlands.

Dissolution of the Monasteries and the Reformation
Acknowledgements

Brocklehurst, Sir Philip (1998), *Swythamley and Its Neighbourhood Past and Present,* Churnet Valley Books; ISBN 1 902685 01 6

Cope, Norman A (1972), *Stone in Staffordshire - The History of a Market Town,* Wood, Mitchell & Co

Durant, David N (1997), *A Historical Dictionary - Life In The Country House,* John Murray; ISBN 0 7195 5075 0

Falkus, Malcolm & John Gillingham (1991), *Historical Atlas of Britain,* Kingfisher Books; ISBN 0 86272 295 0

Hall, Simon & Haywood, John (2001), *The Penguin Atlas of British & Irish History*, Penguin Books Ltd; ISBN 0 140 29518 6

Hey, David ed. (2002), *The Oxford Companion to Local and Family History,* OUP; ISBN 0 19 211688 6

MacCulloch, Diarmaid (2004), *Reformation: Europe's House Divided,* Penguin Books Ltd; ISBN 0140285342

O'Day, Rosemary (1995), *The Longman Companion to the Tudor Age,* Longman; 0582067243

Tomkinson, John L (2000), *Monastic Staffordshire - Religious Houses in Medieval Staffordshire and Its Borderlands*, Churnet Valley Books; ISBN 1897949588

Trevelyan, G M (1986), *English Social History,* Penguin Books Ltd; ISBN 0140099824

The BBC:

http://www.bbc.co.uk/history/state/church_reformation/lollards_01.shtml (accessed 2005)

The Catholic Encyclopedia:

http://www.newadvent.org/cathen/15722a.htm (accessed 2004)

Clarke, Lindsay, British Heritage Magazine/PRIMEDIA Special Interest Publications

Invicta Media:

http://www.theotherside.co.uk/tm-heritage/background/church.htm (accessed 2004)

Sheffield University http://www.shef.ac.uk/uni/academic/A-C/biblst/DJACcurrres/InterestedParties/IntParties7Reformers.pdf (accessed 2005)

Leek Town Guide

David Ross and Britain Express

Appendix 8
Glossary of Terms

Abbreviations in Genealogy and Old Documents

a.	ante, acre
abt.	about
ADC	Aide-de-Camp
adm.	administration, administrator, admitted
admin.	administration, administrator
ae	age, aged
Aff	affidavit
aft.	after
aka	also known as, alias
als	alias
app	appointed
appl.	applied, application
ashlar	a rectangular block of hewn stone used for building purposes
assgn.	assign, assignee
atba	able to bear arms
b.	born
bap.	baptised
bapt.	baptised
Bart	Baronet
bef.	before
beh.	beheaded
beq.	bequest, bequeathed
betw.	between
biog	biography
b-i-l	brother-in-law
BLW	Bounty Land Warrant
b/o	brother of
bo.	boarder
bp.	baptised, birth place
br.	brought, brother
Bt	baronet

bro.	brother
btwn.	between
bur.	buried
c., ca.	circa (about)
capt.	captured, captive
Capt.	Captain
cem.	cemetery
cen.	census
cent.	century
cert.	certificate, certified, certain
cf.	compare
ch.	child
chn	children
chur.	church
chh.	church
cit.	citato (the work cited)
CL	Continental Line
Co.	county, company
coh.	co-heir
Col.	Colonel, Colony
crn.	corner
crenellations	a rampart built around the top of a castle with regular gaps for firing arrows or guns
CS	Civil Service
CSA	Confederate States of America
Ct.	Court
d.	died, days
dau.	daughter
d.c.e.	Writ of "diem clausit extremum" (he has closed his last day)
Dea.	Deacon
dec.	deceased
dec'd, decd.	deceased
dep.	deputy, deposed
depos.	deposed, deposition
div.	divorce(d), division
d/o	daughter of
do.	ditto
dpl	death place

DR	Death Record
Dr.	Doctor
d.s.p./dsp	decessit sine prole (died without issue)
d.s.p. legit/dspl	died without legitimate issue
d.s.p.m./dspm	died without male issue
d.v.p/dvp.	decessit vitae patre (died in father's lifetime)
d.y/dy	died young
dst.	district
e.g.	exempli gratia (for example)
Eng., Engl.	England, English
enl.	enlisted
Ens.	Ensign
est.	estate, estimate
et al	and others
exec.	executor, executed
fam.	family
fB	family Bible
ff.	following
FGS	Family Group Sheets
f-i-l	father-in-law
f/o	father of
FPC	Free Person of Colour
freem.	oath of freeman
frm.	oath of freeman
Ft.	Fort
g.	great
gen.	generation, genealogy, general
Gen.	General (military)
Gent.	Gentleman (a title, not an adjective)
gf.	grandfather
ggf.	great grandfather
gm.	grandmother
ggm	great grandmother
Gov.	Governor
Govt	Government
gr.	grant (as in land), granted
GR	Grave, gravestone
GS	gravestone
h.	husband

Hist.	History, historical, historian
h/o	husband of
Hon.	Honourable (title, not an adjective)
husb.	husband
i.e.	id est (that is)
i.p.m.	Inquisition post mortem
Ibid.	the same
ind.	indictment
inf.	infant, information
Inf.	Infantry
info.	information
inher.	inherited
inst.	instant
int.	interned, interest, marriage intention, interred
inv.	inventory
J.P.	Justice of the Peace
Jr., jun.	junior (younger of two)
j.u.	jure uxoris (right of wife)
k.	killed
K.	King
K.B.	Knight of the Bath
K.G.	Knight of the Garter
kt., knt.	knight
K.T.	Knight of the Thistle (Scotland)
lic.	licence
Lt., Lieut.	Lieutenant
liv.	living (alive), livery
loc. cit.	loco citato (in the place cited)
m., md.	married
m/1 or m1	married first
m/2 or m2	married second
m1 (2)	married first to spouse who was married once before
Maj.	Major
mat.	maternal
matric	matriculated (entered and recorded at college or university)
ment.	mentioned
M.G.	Minister of the Gospel
m-i-l	mother-in-law

mo.	month, mother
M.P.	Member of Parliament, Military Police
MR	marriage record
ms., mss.	manuscript, manuscripts
nd	no date
N.N.	not named (name unknown)
nr.	near
N.S.	New Style date (Gregorian calendar)
nunc.	nuncupative (oral, as opposed to written)
n.x.n.	no Christian name
obit.	obituary
occ.	occupation, occurring
O.E.	Old England/English
op. cit.	opere citato (the work cited above)
ord.	ordained
O.S.	Old Style date (Julian calendar)
p., pp.	page, pages
par.	parent, parish
P.C.	Privy Council
perh.	perhaps
poss.	possibly, possession
pg.	page
pres.	presumed, present
pro.	probated or proved (as in a will)
prob.	probably, probate
propr.	proprietor (land owner)
pub., publ.	published (intent to marry made public)
rec.	record, recorded
ref.	refer, reference
Regt.	Regiment
relecta	widow
relectus	widower
relict	widow/widower
rep.	representative
repud.	repudiated
rem.	removed (moved, left the area)
res.	resides, resided
ret.	retired, returned
Rev.	Reverend

Rot.	rotalus (Roll, Rolls)
s.a.	sine anno (without year)
say	used with a date indicating a great degree of uncertainty (adverb)
s.d.	sine die (without date), step-daughter
sen.	senior (elder of two)
Sr.	Senior
Sergt., Sgt.	Sergeant
serv.	served, servant
sett.	settled, settler
sh.	shortly, ship
sib.	sibling
s-i-l	son-in-law, sister-in-law
sis.	sister
s/o	son of, sister of
sol.	soldier
solar	castle owner's living room and, also, often his bedroom
src.	source
s.s.	step-son
suc.	succeeded (followed)
succ.	successively, succession
summ.	summoned
suo juris	in his (her) right
surg.	surgeon
surv.	survived
twp.	township
ult.	ultimo (last month, as in on the 5th ult.)
unc.	uncle
unk., unkn.	unknown
unm.	unmarried
ux.	uxor or uxoris, wife
v.m./vm	Vita matris (during mother's life)
v.p./vp	Vita patris (during father's life)
vide	see
vol.	volume, volunteer (military)
VR	vital record
w., wf.	wife
wid.	widow
w/o	wife of, never widow of

wd	warranty deed
w.d.	will dated
w.p.	will proved
y.	young, years
yr.	year
yeo	Yeoman

Dictionary & Definitions

Advowson

The right to 'present a living' (appoint a vicar) in the Church of England, belonging to those whose ancestors founded or endowed a church, or to those to whom the right has been transferred. Treated under English civil law as a piece of property which can be transferred by sale or grant.

Alienation

Conveyance of a property to another.

Aristocracy

Some historians use it to describe titled members of society with their families (that is, the nobility) while other historians include both the peerage and the gentry, whether titled or not.

Assart

noun: a piece of land cleared of trees and bushes, and fitted for cultivation.

verb: the act or offence of grubbing up trees and bushes.

Attainder

A penalty by which a person sentenced to death or outlawry on conviction for treason or felony forfeited property and civil rights and 'corruption of the blood' i.e. the attainted person could not inherit nor transmit lands. Bill/Act of Attainder - a legal provision whereby attainder was imposed without court proceedings.

Bordar

A person who was bound to help in the work of the home farm of the lord of the manor – see also 'villein'.

Carucate

The area of land able to be ploughed in a year and a day by a team of eight oxen, which varied between 60 and 180 acres. The average Domesday Book carucate is reckoned to be c 120 acres (48.6 hectares). The carucate is roughly equivalent to the old English unit of land area – the 'Hide' – see later.

Dates

The civil year versus the historical year. In England, from about the late 12th century until 1751, the civil, ecclesiastical and legal year began on 25 March, nearly three months later than the historical year. For dates in the intervening period, the historical year is, therefore, different from the civil year. For example, the date we now call 1 January 1751 (historical year) would be 1 January 1750 (civil year), because the civil year 1750 continued until 24 March. Thus, for dates between 1 January and 24 March, the civil year is one less than the historical year. To avoid confusion, such dates are often written as 1 January 1750-1, or 1 January 1750/1.

Dowager   Originally, a widow with a Dower. The term was later applied to widows of titled men of high rank, to distinguish them from the wives of their sons.

Dower   A widow's life interest in her late husband's estate, for her support and the education of their children: fixed by law at $1/3^{rd}$ of her husband's lands, until abolished in 1925 - see Jointure also.

Dowry   The property in land or money brought by a wife to her husband on marriage; the marriage portion. This was one the ways in which many families increased their wealth and power; in many cases, love was seldom a consideration.

Entail   A system of inheritance through the eldest living, legitimate male heir ('of the body'). As long as there was a male heir, an estate would remain intact, but where the line failed and a daughter inherited, then the estate passed to her husband if or when she had one. The English strict settlement derived from the mediaeval perpetual entail, whereby the succession to an estate was restricted (for example, to the male heirs of the original owner), and the estate could not be disposed of by any life tenant. The perpetual entail was found to be too restrictive and, by the end of the 15th century legal procedures for breaking entails had developed. Between 1500 and 1660, various attempts to restrict rights of alienation and succession were made, often blocked by the courts or by statute, but by 1660, perhaps reflecting a desire for stability of landownership following the English Civil War, the strict family settlement had emerged, with the support of the courts, and this form of landowning predominated until the First World War.

Heirs   Heirs of the Body - descendants of one's bloodline, such as children or grandchildren until such time as there are no direct descendants. If the bloodline runs out, any inheritance will revert to the nearest relative traced back to the original owner.

Heriot   In mediaeval England, a fine payable to the lord of the manor on the death of a person holding land on it e.g. the deceased's best beast or chattel.

Hide   In Anglo Saxon times, the amount of land considered necessary to support a peasant household and allotted to every free householder. The land area varied from 40 to 120 acres.

Hundred   An Anglo Saxon subdivision of an English Shire, being the territory occupied by a hundred families, or which could provide a hundred soldiers or which equalled a hundred Hides.

Jointure   A settlement, on marriage, of lands or income to be held jointly by wife and husband and then, on the husband's death, by the widow. This was an alternative to the widow's rights, under common law, to a dower third of her deceased husband's estate. Property settled on a wife as provision for her widowhood - see Dower also.

Mark   A mediaeval metal unit of accountancy worth 13s 4d (2/3rd of £1). The Mark was much used by appraisers of probate inventories.

Primogeniture   The principle by which the right of inheritance belongs to the eldest son.

Feudal rule of inheritance by which the entire inherited landed estate, excluding only the widow's dower or jointure, passed to the eldest son or, in the absence of sons, to the daughter or daughters (as co-heiresses).

Recusants	A name given in the 16th and 17th century to those who persistently refused to attend Church of England services and so became liable to prosecution under the Acts of Uniformity of 1552 and 1559; the fine of a shilling for each non-attendance was increased to £20 a month in 1581. A further act of 1587 provided for the seizure of two-thirds of the offender's property. Although the measures were initially aimed chiefly at Roman Catholics, Jewish and dissenting Protestant recusants were also punished.
Sequester	To seize a person's property.
Tithe	A tenth part of the produce of land (praedial); of the fruits of labour (personal) and those arising partly out of the ground and partly from work (mixed) offered to the clerical incumbent of a parish benefice. If the incumbent was a rector he would receive the great tithes (wheat, oats etc.) and the small (chickens, goats, lambs etc.) but, when the parish was appropriated, the great tithes fell to the lay impropriator and only the small to the clerical vicar. Some tithes were compounded (i.e. a fixed annual payment was made in lieu of tithe). Others had apparently fallen into disuse. Suits for recovery of tithe filled the ecclesiastical courts during the Tudor period and exacerbated poor relations between clergy and laity as well as between lay impropriators and laymen.
Thegn	An Anglo Saxon thegn or thane was a noble who held his estate on the understanding that in times of war he would fight for the king, be an active member of the witan and undertake duties relating to local and central government. During the reign of the Danish kings the housecarl replaced many of the duties they originally undertook. Following the Norman invasion, the thegn's general affluence diminished due to the practice of splitting the estate between the sons following his death and Norman preferences for their own people.
Villein	A feudal serf. Villeins were tied to the land and could not move away without their lord's consent. They generally rented their own homes but were able to have their own property, unlike

slaves.

Wardship   When a child from a family in England or Wales whose land was held by knight-service was orphaned as a minor, he or she became a royal ward. Until the child came of age the Crown as guardian had rights over the marriage and education of the ward and administered the estates. It was a peculiarly English institution.

Glossary of Terms
Acknowledgements

Durant, David N (1996), *Life in the Country House - A Historical Dictionary,* John Murray; ISBN 0719550750

O'Day, Rosemary (1995), *The Longman Companion to the Tudor Age,* Longman; ISBN 0582067251

The New Penguin English Dictionary, The Penguin Group; ISBN 0140514619; 2001

Appendix 9

Kings, Queens and Rulers of England and Great Britain

This list is intended to give dates of the major royal houses and rulers of England and Great Britain. It is worth noting that Henry II also became King of Ireland in 1172; Wales united with England in 1536-43 and Scotland and England united in 1603:

SAXONS AND DANES

Egbert	827 - 39
Ethelwulf	839 - 58
Ethelbald	858 - 60
Ethelbert	860 - 66
Ethelred I	866 - 71
Alfred *The Great*	871 - 99
Edward *The Elder*	899 - 925
Athelstan	925 - 40
Edmund	940 - 46
Edred	946 - 55
Edwy *The Fair*	955 - 59
Edgar	959 - 75
Edward *The Martyr*	975 - 78

Ethelred II *The Unready*	978 - 1013 & 1014 - 16
Svegn	1013 - 1014
Edmund *Ironside*	1016
Canute (Knut) *the Dane*	1016 - 35
Harold I *Harefoot*	1035 - 40
Hardicanute	1040 - 42
Edward *The Confessor*	1042 - 66
Harold II	1066

NORMAN

William I *The Conqueror*	1066 - 87
William II *Rufus*	1087 - 1100
Henry I *Beauclerk*	1035 - 35
Stephen	1135 - 54

PLANTAGENET

Henry II	1154 - 89
Richard I *The Lionheart*	1189 - 99
John *Lackland*	1199 - 1216
Henry III	1216 - 72
Edward I *Longshanks*	1272 - 1307

Edward II	1307 - 27
Edward III	1327 - 77
Richard II	1377 - 99

LANCASTER

Henry IV *Bolingbroke*	1399 - 1413
Henry V	1413 - 22
Henry VI	1422 - 61 & 1470 - 71

YORK

Edward IV	1461 - 70 & 1471 - 83
Edward V	1483
Richard III *Crookback*	1483 - 85

TUDOR

Henry VII *Tudor*	1485 - 1509
Henry VIII	1509 - 47
Edward VI	1547 - 53
Jane (for only 9 days)	1553
Mary I *Bloody*	1553 - 58

Elizabeth I	1558 - 1603

STUART

James I	1603 - 25
Charles I	1625 - 49

COMMONWEALTH

Commonwealth Council of State	1649 - 53
Oliver Cromwell (Lord Protector)	1653 - 58
Richard Cromwell (Lord Protector)	1658 - 59

STUART RESTORATION

Charles II	1660 - 85
James II	1685 - 88

ORANGE

William III 1689-1702 & Mary II -1694	1689 - 1702

STUART

Anne	1702 - 14

HANOVER

George I	1714 - 27
George II	1727 - 60
George III	1760 - 1820
George IV	1820 - 30
William IV	1830 - 37
Victoria	1837 - 1901

SAXE-COBURG-GOTHA

Edward VII	1901 - 10

WINDSOR

George V	1910 - 36
Edward VIII (325 days)	1936
George VI	1936 - 52
Elizabeth II	1952 -

Appendix 10

The Industrial Revolution and the Development of the Country's Transport Infrastructure

Since Tudor times, parishes had been responsible for ensuring that roads remained passable. Parishioners were charged with the task of providing horses, carts, labour and tools for annual repairs. This arrangement was just about able to cope while road traffic remained localised and there were enough able people and horse teams for the purpose. But despite these endeavours, the roads were little more than the tracks carved out by centuries of localised movements of carts and wagons. The movement of bulky goods by land over longer distances was almost impossible.

Consequently, until the early 18th century, coastal waters provided the most important means of transport of such goods supplemented by those rivers, which were navigable to a greater or lesser degree.

Then came the Industrial Revolution, which began in England in the mid 1700s and acted as a major catalyst for the transport revolution. Besides bringing dramatic changes to modes of transport, the Industrial Revolution brought about great changes in industry, agriculture and society. Because of all the changes during this period, it is sometimes difficult to determine cause and effect. As the transport infrastructure was developed, it was possible for farms, which were becoming more efficient due to increased mechanisation, to support a larger urban population, some of which had been displaced from the countryside. This increasing urban population provided the pool of unskilled workers required by the developing industries of the Industrial Revolution. One of the first industries to benefit from these changes in Great Britain was clothing manufacture (textiles). Such industries are sometimes referred to as trigger industries.

Henry Hobhouse, in his book 'Seeds of Wealth', argues that it is possible that the Industrial Revolution occurred in England fifty to one hundred years ahead of any other country largely because of a national shortage of timber, the first such shortage in a major European power.

Timber supplies had become increasingly insufficient in England at the time of the Reformation. Timber was then used mostly as fuel and, as it became scarce, more and more coal was dug. Coal had been a significant fuel since the early Middle Ages but easily procured surface coal had become deficient. Therefore, coal had to be mined from underground. As mines went deeper, more problems were often experienced with water, which needed to be removed. The answer lay with steam-driven pumps, which, although not very efficient, were in common use more than fifty years before James Watt, who is often credited with the invention of the steam engine. His contribution, albeit a very significant one, was in improving the steam engine's efficiency and reliability.

The largest user of wood in England after domestic purposes was the iron industry, the largest single industrial consumer of fuel in the Western world from early times. In its early days, iron making was a cottage industry using relatively large quantities of wood as charcoal. As early as 1560, the Pagets were involved in iron making on Cannock Chase, as were the Chetwynds, forebears of the Earls of Shrewsbury.[1]

The Reformation had caused a timber shortage in England because Henry VIII had been forced to produce his own cannons and cannon balls as the Emperor Charles V had refused to allow any export of ordnance to his erstwhile Catholic, now Protestant, uncle, who had divorced his aunt, Catherine of Aragon. This forced the English into developing casting techniques for iron cannons, which gave the English an advantage over their continental rivals, who continued using bronze cannons for some time afterwards.

Later, in the 1770s, the dearth of charcoal and, therefore, iron in Britain arose during the American War of Independence, during which European Countries queued up to join the ranks of America's allies and friends. By the end of the war, the Baltic trade was also denied to the British. The coal solution to the shortage of timber (and, therefore of charcoal) was unique to Britain. By the last quarter of the 18th century, the English had learned how to use coke in place of charcoal in the smelting of pure iron.

Coal had the virtue of allowing new industries to grow naturally without always having to re-locate because of wood supplies. Mills were built on every river with sufficient flow and numerous minerals were exploited often in small units. All sorts of industries were built on rivers, which provided both power and the only economic freight transport for both raw materials and finished goods. Initially, road transport did not improve and a town without a nearby river or, later, a canal found itself at a disadvantage. By the end of the 18th century, Staffordshire had become the hub of England's canal system. But, it has already been noted that, as the Industrial Revolution took hold, it forced a dramatic change in the transport infrastructure.

Through the 18th and 19th centuries, several of Staffordshire's aristocracy were very much at the centre of the Industrial Revolution and the associated development of England's transport infrastructure. Included amongst these were some of the families noted in this book e.g. the Littletons/Hathertons - Coal and Canals; the Leveson-Gowers/Egertons/Sutherlands – Coal and Canals; the Pagets/Angleseys – Coal and Canals; the Ryders/Harrowbys - Turnpike Roads. In addition, other Staffordshire noble families, whose lands were located in what is now known as The Black Country, for example, the Wards (Earls of Dudley) and the Legges (Earls of Dartmouth), were involved in these developments.

In the early 18th century, the introduction of and growth in turnpike roads shifted the burden from local parishioners to road users.[2] Tolls were originally based on the size of a vehicle (and number of horses drawing it) or the number of animals in a drove. However, it soon became evident that the size of vehicle was not the only factor in causing damage to road surfaces and Acts were introduced to charge tolls based on the weight of the load and occasionally weighing machines would be built by certain gates. This allowed a ticket to be provided indicating the weight of the vehicle, which could then be produced each time a vehicle passed through a gate subsequently. Turnpike trusts became the institution responsible for administering this innovation, which became a central enabling force in the economic expansion of agriculture and manufacturing. They facilitated the growth of markets, the movement of raw materials and finished goods, and the speedier transmission of news and information. Consequently, transport costs were reduced despite the dislike of the tolls imposed. In fact, there were widespread riots against tolls in 1726. By 1770, there were 15,000 miles of turnpiked roads in England and Wales and during the century as a whole more than 1,000 turnpike acts were passed. This development was stimulated by acceleration of land enclosures, as one of the few obligations the Enclosure Acts [3] imposed on enclosers was the requirement to create a roadway past the newly enclosed meadows. Previously, traffic had simply found its own way across common land by the best available path. In most cases, the Enclosure Acts specified the width of the enclosure roads as forty feet, which gave a traveller a chance of progressing even if it meant weaving from hedge to hedge - metalled roads had not yet arrived!

Although turnpike trusts replaced parishes in maintaining roads, the roads themselves often remained local endeavours - interested local landowners [4] and industrialists frequently subscribed loan funds to the trusts. At first there were no permanent tollhouses and the gates were closed at night, but, once it became apparent that the turnpikes were not temporary, toll houses were built at road junctions with a clear view of the gates and roads. However, there were still complaints that gates were found locked because the keeper was missing or that he was drunk or asleep. The low wages did not always attract decent toll keepers. This changed in the 1770s when the operation of the turnpikes went to the highest bidder at auction (an early example of privatisation). This meant that the successful bidder paid annual rent to the trust, but kept the tolls collected. He would either run the tollgate himself or appoint a gatekeeper.

However, turnpikes remained inadequate for bulky and heavy traffic. Coal and ore were carried by water, which was more practicable and infinitely cheaper. In the 17th and early 18th centuries, a determined effort was made to improve the navigability of rivers but often the courses of the rivers did not suit the transport needs of an economy increasingly based on resources such as coal. The solution lay with canals, also known as deadwater cuts, hence the common expression 'cut' for a canal. The first canals were fundamentally coal canals [5,6], which linked coalfields with ports or navigable water, or with major industrial consumers. Besides those landowners, who had valuable resources under their land, canal building was often promoted by local entrepreneurs [7] who also had much to gain from the speedier circulation of goods and lower transport costs. By the 1830s, Britain had gained some 2,500 miles of canals and navigable rivers.[8]

The age of the canal was relatively short as it was superseded very rapidly by the Railway Age. Although the Stockton to Darlington line carried the first passengers in 1825, the Liverpool & Manchester Railway, which opened on 15 September 1830, was the first commercial passenger line. The London & Birmingham Railway and the Grand Junction Railway quickly followed it. By 1901, the rail network extended to nearly 50,000 miles and, four years later, the Great Western Railway alone carried more freight tonnage than all the inland waterways of Britain put together.

The Railway Age brought about major changes to people's way of life. People travelled further and therefore spent more time on trains. This encouraged entrepreneurs to provide the travellers with something to while away the time during their long journeys; hence the growth of station booksellers.

The Industrial Revolution and the Development of the Country's Transport Infrastructure
Further Notes and Connections

1. See also Note 7 to the chapter: "Here Lies The Leg", which provides a little more detail on the Pagets' iron-making activities.

2. An early Turnpike Act had been passed in 1667. This allowed entrepreneurs to build roads and charge travellers to use the roads in order to defray costs.

3. Between 1750 and 1840, there were around 4,000 Enclosure Acts of Parliament. However, enclosing land was not a new phenomenon; it dated back to at least mediaeval times. Before around 1740, the land around most villages was enclosed by agreement. Often, this involved buying some strips of open fields from the small farmers to remove any possible opposition. Where there was determined opposition from several smaller landowners, an Act of Parliament was needed, which became the accepted procedure after 1750. These acts allowed the whole of a village to be enclosed at the same time instead of piecemeal over a long period of time. Such enclosures, encompassing commons, waste land, meadows and open fields, better defined the patchwork quilt of the countryside as seen so clearly from the air. Nonetheless, even though there have been various bursts of enclosure activity over the centuries, hedges of all dates still exist in England, ranging from Celtic, Saxon, Danish, mediaeval, Tudor, Stuart, Georgian, Victorian to modern times.

4. The 1st Earl of Harrowby at Sandon Hall was an early funder of a turnpike trust, which ran past through his estate and enabled him to supply locally produced goods to the people of the rapidly growing Potteries towns. For more on the Earls of Harrowby, see the chapter: "A Near Escape For a Road Builder".

5. See Note 9 to the chapter: "A Family of Influence", which refers to the Canal Duke, Francis Egerton, the 3rd and last Duke of Bridgewater.

6. See also the chapter: "How To Be Comfortable In Church" and Notes 6 and 11 to the chapter regarding the development of the canal system around Penkridge and the involvement of Sir Edward Littleton.

7.　　An early entrepreneurial promoter of canals in Staffordshire was Josiah Wedgwood, who saw the opportunity to sell his wares to a wider market place.

8.　　In 1699, an Act of Parliament had been passed allowing the 6th Lord Paget to improve the navigation on the River Trent between Burton-on-Trent and Wilden - see also Note 9 of the chapter: "Here Lies The Leg".

The Industrial Revolution and the Development of the Country's Transport Infrastructure
Acknowledgements

Hobhouse, Henry (2003), *Seeds of Wealth,* Macmillan; ISBN 0333903552

The Penguin Atlas of British and Irish History, Penguin Press; ISBN 0140295186; 2001

Gray, Stephane (1995-1997), *Enclosures,* California Polytechnic State University website http://www.cla.calpoly.edu/~lcall/enclosures.html

Further Reading

Hoskins, W.G. (1955), *The Making of the English Landscape*, Hodder & Stoughton; ISBN 0340770201

Appendix 11

Some Introductory Notes to other Staffordshire Families

In the Foreword to this book, I noted that the families discussed had been restricted to those with whom I had been familiar over the years through various interests. I further noted that there were other families, which had been influential in Staffordshire, some of which I referred to by name.

Of these families, the 2nd Lord Wrottesley was a President of the Royal Society and one of the founders of the Astronomical Society. He married Sophia Elizabeth Giffard from Chillington Hall. John Giffard, the current head of the Giffard family, was the Chief Constable of Staffordshire until 2006. The Giffards were also actively involved in aiding Prince Charles (later Charles II) to escape after the Battle of Worcester.

The Sneyds were a well-known North Staffordshire family, who purchased Keele Manor in 1543 for £334 after Henry VIII had seized it in 1540 as part of the Dissolution of the Monasteries. The Sneyds owned Keele until the 20th Century, when Keele Hall and surrounding land was passed on to become the core of what is now the University of Keele.

George Legge, 1st Lord (Baron) Dartmouth, an eminent naval commander, also founded the Royal Fusiliers. His son, William, was created the 1st Earl of Dartmouth in 1711.

Hugo Meynell, who claimed descent from William the Conqueror, later became known variously as both the "father and the king of fox hunting" - after he purchased Quorndon Hall in Leicestershire in 1753, he founded the first and oldest fox-hunt, the Quorn. He later purchased the Staffordshire Hoar Cross estate from the Talbot family and set up the Meynell Hunt. His wife, Elizabeth Ingram-Shepherd, was a daughter of the 9th Viscount Irwin of Temple Newsam House [1] near Leeds. Eventually, their son, Hugo Charles Meynell Ingram, inherited Temple Newsam, as the 9th Viscount died without a male heir and Elizabeth's two elder sisters died without issue. Hugo Charles' elder son,

Hugo Francis Meynell Ingram, died from a hunting accident whilst Master of the Meynell Hunt. He was married to Lady Emily Charlotte Wood, daughter of the 1st Viscount Halifax. Following extensive renovation work, their home, Hoar Cross Hall, is now a world famous Health Spa Resort.

The Bagots of Blithfield Hall have a long association with Staffordshire, as does the Bagot Goat breed, which is believed to come into the possession of the Bagot family sometime in the 14th century. Some of the breed are now kept in the Lake District on the estate, which belongs to another branch of the Bagot family. But that is another story.

Some Introductory Notes to other Staffordshire Families
Further Notes and Connections

1.   Temple Newsam is one of the great historic estates in England. Set within over 1,500 acres of parkland, woodland and farmland landscaped by Capability Brown in the 18th century, it is a magnificent Tudor-Jacobean mansion. It was the birthplace of Lord Darnley, first husband of Mary, Queen of Scots, and home to the Ingram family for over 300 years.

General References & Further Reading
References

Bailie, J M - gen ed (1978), *Hamlyn Dictionary of Dates and Anniversaries,* The Hamlyn Publishing Group; ISBN 0600329275

Cokayne, G E (1982), *The Complete Peerage,* Sutton Publishing; ISBN 0904387828

Cook, Chris (1998), *A Dictionary of Historical Terms,* Macmillan Press; ISBN 0333673484

Danziger, Danny & Gillingham, John (2004), *1215: The Year of Magna Carta,* Coronet Books; ISBN 0340824751

Durant, David N (1996), *A Historical Dictionary: Life in the Country House,* John Murray; ISBN 0719554788

Fraser, Antonia (2004), *The Gunpowder Plot,* Phoenix; ISBN 0753814013

Gardiner, Juliet - ed (2000), *The History Today Who's Who in British History,* Collins & Brown and CiCo Books; ISBN 1855858827

Hicks, Michael (2001), *Who's Who in British History: Late Medieval England 1272-1485,* Stackpole Books; ISBN 0811716384

MacCulloch, Diarmaid (2004), *Reformation: Europe's House Divided 1490-1700,* Penguin Books Ltd; ISBN 0140285342

Montague-Smith ed (1999), *Debrett's Correct Form,* Headline Book Publishing Ltd; ISBN 0747223300

Morgan, John (2001), *Debrett's New Guide to Etiquette & Modern Manners,* Thomas Dunne Books; ISBN 0312281242

Routh, C R N (2001), *Who's Who in British History: Tudor England 1485-*

1603, Stackpole Books; ISBN 0811716392

Thompson, Brian (2002), *Imperial Vanities,* HarperCollins; ISBN 0002571889

Tyerman, Christopher (2001) *Who's Who in British History: Early Medieval England 1066-1272,* Stackpole Books; ISBN 0811716376

The Penguin Atlas of British & Irish History, Penguin Books, ISBN 0140295186; 2001

The Victoria History of the County of Stafford, University of London Institute of Historical Research:

Volume II ISBN 0197227155

Volume IV ISBN 0712910387

Volume VI ISBN 0197227333

Volume XIV ISBN 0197227783

Daily Telegraph - Obituary Pages

Daily Mail

Express & Star

Staffordshire Newsletter

Stafford Post

Whitaker's Almanac

Hull University Archives http://www.hull.ac.uk/arc/ (accessed 2004)

The Catholic Encyclopedia http://www.newadvent.org/cathen/ (accessed 2004/05)

Further Reading

Hobhouse, Henry (1987), *Seeds of Change*, Harper & Row, ISBN 0060914408

Raven, Michael (2005), *A Guide to Shropshire*, Michael Raven, ISBN 0906114349

Raven, Michael (2004), *A Guide to Staffordshire and the Black Country*, Michael Raven, ISBN 0906114330

Salter, Mike (1996), *The Old Parish Churches of Staffordshire*, Folly Publications; ISBN 1871731258

Smith, Peter L (1997), *Discovering Canals in Britain*, Shire Publications Ltd; ISBN 0747802041

Stone, L & J (1986), *An Open Elite? England from 1540 - 1880*, OUP; ISBN 0192851497

Yorke, Trevor (2003), *The Country House Explained*, Countryside Books; ISBN 1853067938

Yorke, Trevor (2004), *The English Abbey Explained*, Countryside Books; ISBN 1853068543

Turner, E S (2003), *Amazing Grace – The Great Days of Dukes*, Sutton Publishing, ISBN 0750932724

The Diaries of The First Lord Hatherton - Extracts (2003); Cromwell Press - originals held at the Staffordshire Records Office, Stafford

INDEX

Noble Curios and Connections
Index

ISBN 141209334-1

9 781412 093347